Card

I am Mary, I am woman

THEOLOGICAL AND ANTHROPOLOGICAL APPROACHES TO THE PEOPLES' MARY

the columba press

First published in 2010 by
the columba press
55A Spruce Avenue, Stillorgan Industrial Park,
Blackrock, Co Dublin

Cover by Bill Bolger
The cover photograph is by Fr Gareth Byrne
Origination by The Columba Press
Printed in Ireland by ColourBooks Ltd, Dublin

ISBN 978 1 85607 710 1

Contents

Acknowledgements

This book would not have been possible without the wise counsel, energetic debates and invaluable assistance of my good friends and colleagues in Mater Dei Institute of Education, St Patrick's College, Drumcondra and Dublin City University. I am very grateful for their patience and encouragement and in particular for those who read or advised me on specific sections of the text relevant to their fields of discipline. They include Dr Dermot Lane, President of Mater Dei Institute, Dr Kevin Williams, Dr Ethna Regan, Dr James O'Higgins Norman, Dr Will Murphy, Dr Gabriel Flynn, Dr Fearghus Ó Fearghail, Dr Eoin Cassidy, Dr Chris O'Donnell O Carm, Mr Peter Folan his library staff and Ms Semra Abdulahovic. In addition, for their support and encouragement, I should like to thank Ms Carol Barry, Ms Anne Hession, Dr Niamh Middleton, Fr Fachtna McCarthy, Ms Cora O'Farrell and finally from York St John University, Dr Chris Maunder.

The writing of a book does not come without its sacrifices most of which are experienced by the long absences of the author in relation to family and friends. I wish, therefore, to thank my much loved brothers and sisters Tom, Tilda, Valentine, Anne, my sister-in-law Caroline and nephews and nieces for understanding the necessity of my infrequent visits to Glasgow, not excluding my old and dear friends in that city Mgr Peter O'Farrell, Ms Mary Margaret Cosgrove, Ms Eileen Buchanan McLoone, Ms Margaret Kelly and Ms Sadie Brooks-Jeffrey. A special word of thanks goes also to my Dublin friends Ms Diane O'Farrell on the thirtieth anniversary of our friendship and to Ms Kathriona Murphy.

Finally, and most especially I am eternally grateful to Mr Seán O Boyle of The Columba Press for his personal kindness and professional interest in the publication of this work. Ultimately, it is the confidence of the publisher that makes it all possible.

Introduction

So I turned to consider wisdom and madness and folly ...
then I saw that wisdom excels folly as light excels darkness.
The wise man has his eyes in his head but the fool walks in
darkness (Ecclesiastes 2:12-14).

It would be unusual to introduce a book with an extract taken
from a scriptural text that tends to be viewed as fatalistic. Still
the philosopher-author Qoheleth's realistic reflection on life signals
the challenge to anyone who ventures yet another exposition into
the most complex expressions of symbolic womanhood Christendom has ever known; Mary the Mother of God. If we incorporate
into that equation the modern view of human anthropology
from a Christian feminist perspective, then we are left with a
question posed by Qoheleth's own rhetoric: 'Then I said to
myself, what happens to the fool will happen to me also; why
then have I been so very wise?' (Eccles 2:12-13). Some may
believe that to embark on such an enterprise requires of the
theologian all the elements of wisdom, madness and folly, and
not without good reason. Firstly, writing a treatise on Mary of
Nazareth that is inclusive enough to satisfy the full meaning
behind the doctrines, images and practices attaching to her two-
thousand year old persona will bear only limited fruit. Secondly,
to explore Marian theology as a possible means of mediation
conversant with both Catholic Church teaching and Christian
feminist anthropology may seem unachievable.

Nonetheless, the two-fold rationale for this short volume is
to pursue just such a task. Firstly, the primary objective is to
propose a new methodology in order to categorise the complex
nature of some of the material as it is found in the long centuries
of Marian tradition. The methodology does not aspire to a
definitive categorisation of Mary's role and function. Rather it
suggests that the constant, eternal presence and figure of Mary
for Catholic Christians may be subsumed into three broad
Marian typologies, namely Mary as *Theatype*, Mary as *Christatype*

and Mary as *Ecclesiatype*. Each of these types iis consistent with a
tradition which attempts to encapsulate some of the diverse
beliefs and images of the Marian mystery through the
devotional and theological aproaches of her followers past and
present. To put it simply, Mary has a personal and communal
story and one which many want to be part of from their own
particular perspective. Some, for example, would put Mary on a
very high pedestal, perhaps too high. This is the theatypical
approach (Mary as Theatype) which verges on virtual worship
of her, coming close to the kind of honour that would be
reserved for God alone. Mary as Theatype is neither known nor
condoned in any official documents of the tradition. However,
this type reveals some evidence that Mary of Nazareth has been
exalted to near God-like status variously throughout the
centuries by members of the faithful, often through exaggerated
piety or popular devotion.

Keeping in mind that none of the three typological approaches
is necessarily exclusive of the other, there are those who would
follow the christatypical approach (Mary as Christatype),
placing her in close proximity to Christ where she stands at her
Son's side with the power to co-redeem, co-mediate and to act as
intercessor between humankind and God. Yet others again
would prefer the ecclesiatypical approach (Mary as Ecclesiatype) which images her from the perspective of her own
humanity and in that respect Mary is uniquely present to them,
the church as the People of God. These latter two types are
based upon usage of the words 'christotypical and ecclesiotypical'[1] employed around the time of the Second Vatican
Council to emphasise both the christological and ecclesiological
aspects of Mary's role in Catholic Christianity. It should be
noted that the relatively sparse and undeveloped use of those
two terms has made it possible to take the liberty of changing
and developing them quite radically in the construction of the
Marian methodology being proposed here.

In light of the various interpretations of the purpose of a
'typology', some clarification as to its meaning is required in

---

1. See Anthony Tambasco, *What are they saying about Mary?* New York:
Paulist Press, 1984, p 32

relation to the Marian types where, in this instance, Otto Semmelroth presents an acceptable framework. He explains that a typology has the ability to contain a three-fold symbolism. Firstly, it may refer to the personification or representation of a spiritual entity through some kind of image. Secondly, it can point to a real bond between one entity and another as the objective foundation of that relationship and, thirdly, 'it can be a moral example as a result of this relationship'.[2] Using Semmelroth's understanding, it may be claimed that the three Marian types are truly typologies since: (i) Mary has the capacity to personify or be a representative of God, Christ and the church; (ii) there can be little doubt that there is a real bond between Mary, God, Christ and the church; (iii) Mary can be taken as the moral example of one who has an ontological relationship with God, Christ and the church.

The second objective of this volume is to show how the Marian types have the capacity to generate substantial theological agreement between traditional Catholic Church teaching and Christian feminist hermeneutics. In particular, this will be demonstrated in the magisterial documents of the Second Vatican Council, Pope Paul VI and Pope John Paul II and in the writings of a number of feminist theologians. To this end, the fourth chapter will offer a perspective on the difficulties that many women have encountered in the tradition. For example, that chapter will raise in particular the problem of the non-ordination of women, theological disquiet about the patriarchal structures of the church, and explain how these and related matters are perceived to be at odds with the values of the gospels. This takes place primarily in the interest of sustained theological debate and always in search of a gender inclusive forum on matters of the utmost importance to the entire faith community.

---

2. Otto Semmelroth, *Mary the Archetype of the Church*, Dublin: Gill and Son, 1964, p 28

CHAPTER ONE

They Called Her God?

Men give to her the jewelled crown, and robe with broidered rim,
But she is fain to cast them down because of Him.[1]

Mary as Theatype

'Oh we have never called her God!' we cry. It is unlikely that anyone who has ever professed to be a member of the Catholic Church would admit to the heretical deviation of exalting Mary of Nazareth to near God-like status. Yet, such was the outpouring of devotion to her at times throughout the long centuries of Christianity that her images tended to soar to a comfortable resting place close to the Godhead. Imaging Mary to such excessive extent will be referred to below as the theatypical approach to Mariology. Nor is it difficult to perceive how that approach came about. According to the gospels of Luke (1:26-38) and Matthew (1:18-25), the impossible happened where Mary, without recourse to copulation, miraculously conceived the Son of God in her womb. The apocryphal *Proto-evangelium* or the Gospel of James (c. AD150) portrays her as a very special, precocious child prepared in readiness for the greatest of all mysteries which she would soon experience. Here Mary excelled in every way in her knowledge, her unique physical purity and as a result of the miraculous choosing of Joseph for her as a husband from an assembly of widowers. The apocryphal accounts of Mary's early life do not belong to the canon of the scriptures such as Luke and Matthew, nor are they specifically theologically significant. Nonetheless they exercised a considerable influence on certain controversies and devotion which traversed the centuries through the media of tradition, myth and legend.

The theatypical approach is about the deification of Mary which is sometimes obscured and sometimes disclosed particularly

---

1. Geoffrey Anketell Kennedy,'Good Friday Falls on Lady Day', *The Unutterable Beauty*, London: Hodder and Stoughton, 1947, p 98

in popular piety, but it has existed and its vestiges remain in modern times. Maurice Hamington comes close to expressing that phenomenon when he says that Mary 'became an objectified reality of mythic proportions in the early church. She was subsequently reified on an unofficial level by the faithful who adored her, and was later reified on a dogmatic level through the infallible papal pronouncements.'[2] Although the church's Marian doctrines never proclaimed Mary's role to be of god-like status, church teaching unintentionally colluded with excessive popular devotion through its dogmatic statements, all of which gathered momentum as the centuries of Catholic Christianity progressed. The theatypical approach arises from that accumulation of emotional and spiritual beliefs about Mary. These coupled with audacious, polemical debates propelled this woman of Nazareth from relative obscurity in the New Testament to a pseudo-goddess of idolatrous proportions. It is Mary's towering and ubiquitous presence that leads us to an exploration of her having been imaged variously as the greatest female deity of all time.

The term to describe these phenomena – Mary as Theatype - is not found in the tradition but originates here to illustrate how mariology was to give rise to mariolatry. We begin by uncovering the origin of the theatypical approach, the ancient Mother Goddess and the development of a number of themes and elements which, through misappropriation of their use, have contributed to the creation of the typology. Primarily, these include the ancient title of *Theotokos*, the dogma of the Immaculate Conception, Mary's virginal motherhood and specific aspects of her relationship with the Holy Spirit.

The Theatype Emerging
The case for Mary being imaged as Theatype is reflected in the ancient Mother Goddess, the matrix from which everything in existence emerges. Most cultures in history, whether mono-theistic or polytheistic, have had a female figure that represents and embodies the role of motherhood. To the Egyptians she was Isis, to the Romans she was Kybele or the *Magna Mater*, to the

---

2. Maurice Hamington, *Hail Mary?* New York: Routledge, 1995, p 25

Greeks she was *Rhea*, in Hinduism she is *Kali, Parvati* and *Durga*, for the Buddhists she is *Bodhisattava* or *Quan Yin*, in Islam she is Maryam, the mother of the prophet Isa and in Christianity she is known as the Virgin Mary, Mother of God Incarnate. Although Christianity does not equate Mary with any of the numerous forms of these mother goddesses, early Christians appropriated many of them into the personhood of the Mother of God. As Christianity advanced, Mary's image became ever more reflective of the ancient Egyptian Goddess Isis and the symbol of universal motherhood. Isis-worship spread throughout the Greco-Roman world where she was celebrated as the ideal mother and wife, patron of nature and magic, and friend of slaves and sinners. She heard the supplications and prayers not only of the downtrodden but also the wealthy, maidens and aristocratic rulers. A familiar depiction of Isis was that of her in a sitting position with Horus her son on her knee. The icon of Isis and Horus was transferred to the Madonna and Child where, in earlier representations of these latter carvings, it was almost impossible to tell which pair was which.[3]

It is proposed here that this 'replacement' phenomenon, compounded by centuries of accrual of representations, images, doctrines, dogmas and privileges, gathered momentum in the minds of the faithful until it eventually reached its crescendo in Mary being imaged as possessing deified status. Although he barely hints at this suggestion, scripture scholar John McKenzie claims that the lack of historical evidence in the New Testament gave rise to a devotion which became entirely unrestrained.[4] This kind of Marian devotion appears to have found its source among the Collyridians (AD375), an obscure minor early Christian heretical group of which little is now known. Geoffrey Ashe says that this sect represented a parallel Marian religion to Christianity founded by first-generation followers of the Virgin Mary. It is possible that their doctrines were later subsumed by

3. Ishara, 'The Virgin Mary Isis of the Third Millennium'?? [online] http://www.angelfire.com/realm2/amethystbt/MaryIsis.html [Accessed 19 October 2007].
4. John McKenzie, 'The Mother of Jesus in the New Testament', *Concilium*, Vol 168, (1983), p 9

the church at the Council of Ephesus (AD431) where she was eventually proclaimed *Theotokos* (God-Bearer).[5] Now we see the seeds of imaging Mary as Theatype emerging through a form of excessive devotion manifesting itself in the theatypical approach.

The Theatypical Approach

Even before the decree of the Council of Ephesus, Mary's elevation was discernible in the devotion of the grassroots faithful. According to Charlene Spretnak, during the first several centuries of Christianity the laity intuited an elemental mystical engagement between Christ and Mary due to his *mystical* birth.[6] Spretnak goes incredibly far in her own account of what that 'mystical engagement' between Mother and Son actually means. Relying on twenty-first century understanding of physiology, she holds that Mary's body must have contained DNA (deoxyribonucleic acid) cells of God-the-Son from the moment of his conception to the end of her life. With the entry of the DNA cells into her womb, God in both human *and divine* form gestated in Mary. That phenomenal mystery of the relationship between Mary and the Second Person of the Blessed Trinity is expressed by Spretnak accordingly:

> Moreover, contemporary science tells us that pregnancy and child-birth alter the mother's brain by creating new neural pathways. Imagine the neural pathways that would develop in a woman's brain while God-the Son was gestating within her and growing from her very flesh! Of course, Jesus was physiologically fully human, but he was also fully divine – and they both knew that, which surely must have lent a profound dimension to their intimate connection.[7]

Spretnak's extraordinary 'gestation theory' bestows upon Mary an incredible image of one who possesses esoteric power within the Godhead through her understanding of the elemental

5. Geoffrey Ashe, *The Virgin: Mary's Cult and the Re-Emergence of the Goddess*, London: Arkana, 1985, p 151
6. Charlene Spretnak, *Missing Mary*, New York: Palgrave Macmillan, 2004, p 208
7. Spretnak, *Missing Mary*, p 208

connection between Mother and Son that remained with Mary
for all time and eternity. She criticises what she refers to as
Vatican II 'progressives' for having, 'no reason to think Mary
was ontologically changed by bearing God-the-Son, and,
therefore no reason to think she grew to have more-than-human
capabilities'.[8] As far as Spretnak is concerned there must be no
further shrinking of Mary's significance in Catholic Christianity.
It is time for her to make her return and revisit 'that which is
nearly lost but might be saved if the Marian resurgence continues
to gain strength'.[9] Return we now will to account for the devotion,
perchance it could be ventured even worship of her, that
manifested itself in the theatypical approach through the
centuries in popular piety. Praise of Mary is perhaps the most
perplexing phenomenon of all Marian theology, for where is the
line to be drawn between an acceptable form of devotion and an
excessive form of worship? As John Macquarrie expresses it:

> How does one distinguish between genuine development of
> a doctrine, the drawing out of truths concealed in the original,
> from illegitimate accretions which get added by later gener-
> ations but may be quite at variance with the intention of the
> original affirmations from which they claim to be derived?[10]

Certainly, the church's dictum on *Latria, Hyperdulia* and *Dulia*
(respectively the supreme adoration offered to God alone, the
degree of veneration given to Mary alone and a lesser veneration
paid to the angels and saints) offers clear guidelines. Nonetheless, licence has often been taken with church dictates and in
reference to *Latria* and *Hyperdulia* the guiding principles have
sometimes been blurred if not, indeed, distorted. Imaging Mary
as Theatype is one such example where those who follow the
'theatypical approach' lean considerably closer to *Latria* than to
Hyperdulia. The theatypical approach falls just short of worship
of Mary, but can it be seriously asserted that this is a valid claim?
Certainly the scriptures do not tender any such indication.
Rather, tradition and popular piety are much more likely to
have been the primary movers. In Christianity, the Council of

8. Spretnak, *Missing Mary*, p 208
9. Spretnak, *Missing Mary*, p 25
10. John Macquarrie, *Mary for all Christians*, London: Collins, 1991, p 48

Ephesus (AD431) using the title *Theotokos* albeit unwittingly, wedged open the door for veneration of Mary gradually leading to her pseudo-goddess-status image. Even when early church teaching made efforts to keep control over devotion to her, popular piety elevated Mary far beyond the intention of the church fathers' doctrinal statements.[11] Popular piety, acting on the official *Theotokos* title, contributed to Mary's elevation and the developing of dramatic ideas about her role in Catholic Christianity.

Mary as Theotokos

According to Juan Luis Bastero, 'The mystery of Mary's divine motherhood constitutes her *raison d'être*, the deepest explanation of her life and of the place she occupies in God's plan of salvation. Her divine motherhood is, in effect, the central mystery of our Lady's life, on which are based all the other mysteries connected with her'.[12] Although it was the development of the title *Theotokos* more than anything else that contributed to the rise of Mary's theatypical status, her role as the Mother of God is not the issue of itself. Rather it is the way in which she has been portrayed as a result of the misuse of the *Theotokos* title in the tradition. A summary sketch of how that tradition originated and developed as a reminder of its importance is deserving of some consideration presently.

Irenaeus the Bishop of Lyon (d.c. AD200) expressed his belief in Mary's divine motherhood in terms which anticipated Mary as *Theotokos*. Michael O'Carroll's interpretation of these terms is found in phrases which he extracted from Irenaeus. They are as follows:

'The Son of God was born of the Virgin'. In dealing with the virginal conception, on which he [Irenaeus] insisted often, he invokes Old Testament texts and figures. Adam was fashioned from the'virgin earth', a type of the virgin birth. Is 7:14 was especially related to the Virgin Mary. The stone cut

---

11. Rosemary Ruether, *Mary – The Feminine Face of the Church*, London: Westminster Press, 1977, pp 60-61.
12. Juan Luis Bastero, *Mary Mother of the Redeemer*, Dublin: Four Courts Press, 2006, p 154

by no human hands in Dan 2:34 was also a type of her motherhood, with which text [Irenaeus] linked Is 28:16. On Gen 3:15 ... he is quoted as the first of the Fathers to interpret the oracle in a Marian sense, but he does so in the context of a collective meaning, with the conflict between the demon and the descendants of Eve, the triumph won by Christ, born of the Virgin Mary.[13]

At this early stage of Christianity, Irenaeus was only hinting at Mary as *Theotokos*, using the virginal conception as a means to do so. Mary is simply seen as the foundation of Jesus' coming into the world. She is the virgin who gave birth to the Son of God, not of any man but by the overshadowing of the Spirit. She alone as Virgin Mother is the cornerstone and foundation for the special Child. The tradition was at too early a stage for Irenaeus to have claimed any more. Nonetheless, he laid the ground for the theology of the subsequent Greek and Latin fathers of the church.

The real debate on the divine maternity is due in no small measure to one Cyril the Bishop of Alexandria (c. AD375-444). He was the key figure responsible for the official pronouncement on Mary as *Theotokos* which was proclaimed at Ephesus (AD431). This came about as the result of a controversy between Cyril and Nestorius, a Syrian monk, the latter having been appointed as Patriarch of Constantinople (c. AD386-451) by the Emperor Theodosius II (AD428). Although the term had been in existence for well over a century, the debate itself only came to a head when Cyril and Nestorius quarrelled.[14] The risk of promoting the *Theotokos* title at this time had to be given careful consideration through certain fear that God born from woman might be associated with Mary's precursors such as Isis and Kybele – mothers of the gods. When a preacher who was known to Nestorius sermonised against proclaiming Mary, a mere human, as *Theotokos* (Bearer of God), Nestorius felt impelled to draw a distinction between that quarrel and another which asserted that Mary could not possibly be anymore than *Anthropotokos* (mother of the man Jesus). By way of compromise,

13. Michael O'Carroll, *Theotokos*, Wilmington: Glazier, 1982, p 190
14. Dermot Lane, *The Reality of Jesus*, Dublin: Veritas, 1975, pp 100-104

Nestorius proposed an earlier formulation *Christotokos* (Bearer of Christ) by Theodore of Mopsuestia (d. 427) but this was not to make for peace. Nestorius subsequently condemned the use of the *Theotokos* title, creating for himself an arch opponent in Cyril of Alexandria.

Cyril of Alexandria, on the other hand, followed arguments from the tradition of the church challenging anyone to doubt the Holy Virgin to be the *Theotokos*. When Cyril appealed to Pope Celestine I charging Nestorius with heresy, the matter was then resolved at the First Council of Ephesus (AD431) at the Church of Mary in Ephesus, Asia Minor. The Pope agreed and gave Cyril his authority to serve Nestorius with a notice to recant his views or else face excommunication. Before the summons arrived, Nestorius convinced the Emperor Theodosius II to hold a general council for further debate. Approximately 250 bishops were present. The proceedings were conducted in a heated atmosphere of confrontation and recriminations. Unfortunately, it has to be said that some skulduggery was afoot particularly if a historical account of the times, according to Miri Rubin, is true:

> Cyril mustered the considerable resources – financial as well as diplomatic – of the see of Alexandria and put them to work. He drafted a memorandum to his supporters in Constantinople with a list of sweeteners, gifts and outright bribes to ladies-in-waiting and eunuchs of the imperial court, in an attempt to prevent any backsliding on Mary as *Theotokos*. Luxuries fit for an imperial household, home of the emperor's sisters, were bestowed: 77,760 gold pieces, twenty-four carpets, twenty-five woollen tapestries, twenty-four silken veils, twenty eight cushions, and thirty-six throne covers … Pulcheria, the eldest sister of Theodosius II's sisters, took a vow of virginity, and thus positioned herself most aptly as a special devotee of Mary. She founded churches and endowed them with precious gifts … According to a sympathiser of Nestor, Cyril was 'working on the sister' with Egyptian flatteries. At stake were issues of decorum, related to the appropriate place of women in the imperial cult around Mary … Nestor ended his days in exile.[15]

15. Miri Rubin, *Mother of God a History of the Virgin Mary*, London: Allen Lane, 2009, p 47

This Council of Ephesus subsequently condemned Nestorius and accepted the teaching of Cyril of Alexandria which is church doctrine up until the present day.[16] Nestorius was officially condemned on two counts. Firstly, because he refused to accept that the Son of God was born of the Virgin Mary, suffered died and rose again. Secondly, not only did he refuse to accept Mary as the Mother of God, *Theotokos*, but he also failed to acknowledge the human and the divine in the person of Jesus.[17] As Sarah Boss explains:

> The main weakness of Nestorius's position was that it could not account adequately for the union of divinity and humanity in Christ, and gave the impression that the divinity and humanity were in some way stuck together without being properly united. If Mary did not give birth to God, then how and when did the Word of God unite himself to Christ's humanity? ... Cyril, by contrast, argued that the child to whom Mary gave birth was the one in whom 'the Word was flesh', and this made it clear that, in Christ, the two could not be separated.[18]

It is interesting to note that huge crowds had gathered in the streets of Ephesus awaiting the result of the debate. When they heard that Cyril had been successful, they were excited enough to carry him and his bishops through the streets in torchlight procession from their meeting place. The bishops had met in the Marian church built near the ancient temple of the goddess Diana whose religion had been suppressed by the Emperor Theodosius the Great – fifty years before. It is also noteworthy that in the same city Paul of Tarsus in his day had been shouted down when he threatened the livelihood of the Ephesian worshippers of the goddess Artemis. Reference to that fact is found in the New Testament Acts:

> A certain silversmith named Demetrius made silver models of the temple of the goddess Artemis, and his business

---

16. John Paul II, *Mulieris Dignitatem*, Dublin: Veritas, 1987, par 4
17. Lane, *The Reality of Jesus*, p 102
18. Sarah Boss, 'The Title Theotokos' in S. Boss (ed), *Mary the Complete Resource*, New York: Oxford University Press, 2007, p 54

brought a great deal of profit to the workers ... Now, you can see and hear for yourselves what this fellow Paul is doing. He says that man-made gods are not gods at all, and he has succeeded in convincing many people, both here and in Ephesus and in nearly the whole province of Asia. There is the danger, then, that this business of ours will get a bad name. Not only that, but there is also the danger that the temple of the great goddess Artemis will come to mean nothing and that her greatness will be destroyed – the goddess worshipped by everyone in Asia and in all the world! (Acts 19: 24-27).

It might not stretch the imagination too far to suggest that the veneration of a mother-figure was ingrained in the hearts of the Ephesians by the time of the Council of Ephesus. One could perhaps even claim that the populace now had their goddess back in the guise of Mary the Mother of God. Spretnak maintains that the declaration of the *Theotokos*, 'was responsible more than any other clerical intervention in the history of the church for officially enlarging the role and perception of Mary of Nazareth. All subsequent elevations of the Virgin follow from this decision.'[19]

Theotokos *and the Theatype*

From Ephesus onwards the theatypical approach begins to emerge as a consequence of the *Theotokos* title. However, at this early stage there is still a notable distinction between devotion to Mary and the greater worship given to her Son. Any attempt on the part of the populace to move from devotion to worship was kept in check officially. Often this was due to the fact that many of the early fathers of the church had to cope with heresies such as the worship of the pagan goddesses, whoever or wherever they happened to manifest themselves at the time. It must be said, nonetheless, that although it was easy enough for the learned fathers to teach that Mary was the Mother of God, it was much more difficult for a simple Christian people surrounded by various pagan religions, complete with their own goddesses, to comprehend the nuances.

---

19. Spretnak, *Missing Mary*, p 153

Undoubtedly various translations through the ages added to this complex mystery which must seem to beg the question, 'Which comes first, the chicken or the egg?' If Mary is the Mother of God, then in the nature of things she must have been born before God. On the other hand, how is it possible for her to be the Mother of God if she were one of God's creatures? The answer, of course, is that Mary is not the Mother of God but the Mother of God Incarnate in Jesus the Christ. This important point is seldom portrayed in literary translations. Neither the English (Mother of God) nor the Latin (*Mater Dei*) normally includes the term 'incarnate'. Such is the case even in official documents today. In other words, Mary should not to be imaged solely as the Mother of God. Rather, she is to be understood as the Mother of God Incarnate or *Mater Dei Incarnati*. The Greek *Theotokos* is translated generally as 'God-bearer'.

Doubtless then that the early fathers had difficulty in separating their teaching of Mary as Mother of God from the emerging theatypical image of Mary as goddess, a connection not too far removed from many of her devoted faithful. Spretnak is close to the mark when she says that, then as now, 'The laity precede the hierarchy in perceiving an expanded sense of Mary's spiritual presence and the increased honour it evokes.'[20] Shortly before the Council of Ephesus, Epiphanius (d. AD403) had one such problem with the Collyridians (mentioned above) mostly consisting of women who represented a parallel Marian religion to Christianity. Although the evidence is scant, it is believed that they sought to deify and offer worship to Mary. Furthermore it was supposed that at their liturgical services they submitted bread to her as a sacrifice and were evidently influenced by contemporary pagan customs. Epiphanius writes, 'Certain women adorn a chair or a square throne, spread a linen cloth over it, and on a certain day of the year place bread on it and offer it in the name of Mary, and all partake of this bread'[21] – a practice which Epiphanius refutes on

---

20. Spretnak, *Missing Mary*, p 153
21. Epiphanius, *Panarion* in Philip R. Amidon (ed), *The Panarion of St Epiphanius, Bishop of Salamis: Selected Passages 79.1., 79.9.3*, Oxford: Oxford University Press, 1990, pp 353-354

the grounds that no woman can exercise priestly functions not even Mary herself.

One of the most influential figures of the fourth-century was Ambrose, Bishop of Milan (d. AD397) and a Latin Father of the Church who also had to develop his doctrine of Mary against the pagan worship of the Great Mother Kybele. She was known as the *Magna Mater*, Mother of the gods where her worship had spread throughout the Roman Empire. She was a goddess of the earth in its primitive state who ruled over wild beasts, mountains and caverns and the celebration of her festival was found on the Roman calendar. Along with her consort, the vegetation god Attis, Kybele was worshipped in wild, emotional, bloody, orgiastic, invigorating ceremonies. Since the danger of elevating Mary to the level of goddess was so great while the cult of Kybele was still flourishing, Ambrose had an aversion to using either of the terms *Mater Dei Incarnati* or *Theotokos*.

Ambrose's tribulations were compounded by the heresy of Arius of Antioch (c. AD250-336) who argued for Jesus' dependence on God the Father, distinguishing between God and the Son whom God had created. Although Ambrose establishes with absolute certainty Mary's divine motherhood, he guards against any idea that might lead the faithful, desperate no doubt for a feminine divinity, to believe as much. He explains that, 'Christ could not, however, have a mother according to his divine nature, because he is his mother's Creator. He was made, not by divine, but rather by human generation. Because he was made man, God was born.'[22]

Ambrose's well known phrase, 'Mary was the temple of God, not the God of the temple'[23] sums up the dilemma encountered by the church fathers as they tried to keep excessive elevation of Mary under control. Never at any stage in this early tradition is she recognised by the fathers as someone who is worshipped in her own right. The most she receives is a superlative form of devotion, but the line is a fine one, with attempts at worship of Mary continuing to wax and wane until the early Middle Ages.

---

22. Ambrose, 'On the Death of His Brother Satyrus' in Deferrari (ed) *Fathers* 22, Washington DC: The Catholic University of America Press, 1968, p 166
23. Ambrose, 'The Holy Spirit' in Deferrari (ed) *Fathers* 22, Washington DC: The Catholic University of America Press, 1963, p 181

The Theatype Developing

However, it must be reiterated at this juncture that the excessive devotion to Mary, which began to establish itself around the tenth century, was not officially escalated by official church teaching. Nor can it be claimed that those who imaged Mary as Theatype were necessarily theologians of renown. Nonetheless, some of them were important men and not without considerable influence over multitudes of the faithful in Christendom. The habitual use of the title *Theotokos* by church theologians unintentionally encouraged a devotion to Mary that slowly escalated until it reached a crescendo during the Middle Ages. Imaging Mary as Theatype is the kernel of the theatypical approach where the powerful Emperor Leo VI (d. AD912), for example, left aside his affairs of state to engage in writing mariology. Focusing on the *Theotokos* in one of his writings, he made a point of claiming that Mary was not created entirely from flesh and blood. He describes her as the lily among thorns in the midst of human wickedness and confusion. Up until the time of her existence, he claimed poetically that the earth only produced thorns but now it has produced fruit. However, although she was still capable of assisting those in need, Mary became estranged from the earth because she could not bear to be separated from her Son.[24] We begin to see at this stage an understanding of Mary's removal from her earthly status towards a more ethereal one.

Leo VI is followed by another influential exponent of elevated mariology, John the Geometer, a monk-priest and archbishop of his time (d. AD990). What is noteworthy is the Geometer's understanding of the part played by Mary in the redemption, which seems to supersede that of Christ's. It is almost as if he is pushed aside with Mary surpassing him in the role of redemption. The Geometer expresses his innermost thoughts even as he prays to Christ:

> ... that you [Christ] have not only given yourself as a ransom for us, but, after yourself, have given also your mother as a ransom at every moment, so that you indeed have died for us once, but she died a million times in her will, cauterised in

24. Cited in Graef, *Mary*, Vol 1, pp 194-195

her heart just as for you, so also for those for whom she, just like the Father, has given her own Son and knew him to be delivered unto death.[25]

The implication of this statement indicates that Mary is almost as close to God in her suffering as is Christ, if not more so. In this respect, as in others such as intelligence and under-standing, she is far above all the heavenly creatures, being sweet, frightening and invisible all at one and the same time. Mary now no longer bears any resemblance to the young girl who gave birth to the baby Jesus in Bethlehem.

By the thirteenth-century, evidence of Mary as Theatype becomes evermore apparent with Richard of St Laurent (d. AD 1245) who goes far in asserting that Mary's place is within the Godhead. Of his Marian doctrine and devotion he writes, 'Our Mother who art in heaven, give us our daily bread.'[26] Clearly he sees Mary as the feminine face of God and an entity of the Trinity. Furthermore, he writes, 'Mary so loved the world, that is sinners, that she gave her only-begotten Son for the salvation of the world.'[27] This theme originates in the gospel of John, ('for) God so loved the world that he gave his only Son, so that everyone who believes in him may not perish but may have eternal life' (Jn 3:16). Richard images Mary as one who is omnipotent on earth, heaven and hell. As she is Queen of these three realms, she is equal to the King where her powers manifest themselves through her ability to free those already in the devil's clutches. She can return lost souls back to life so that they may do repentance for their evil wrongdoings. Here again Mary is in a position not only to implore Christ to save the world but also to command him to do so by her maternal authority.[28]

Another example of the imaging of Mary as Theatype during the Middle Ages is found in Bernardine of Siena (d. AD1444) who was a popular preacher at the time. His theatypical approach reached incredible heights. Even when she was in the womb of her mother, Mary was in possession of her own free

25. Cited in Graef, *Mary*, Vol 1, pp 197-198
26. Cited in Graef, *Mary*, Vol 1, p 266
27. Cited in Graef, *Mary*, Vol 1, p 266
28. Cited in Graef, *Mary*, Vol 1, p 269

will. From the moment of the annunciation, she was so
advanced in her knowledge that she was completely conversant
with the mystery of the incarnation. Not only did he believe that
she supplanted Christ, but Mary, in some respects, became
superior even to the God-Self. The quotation below reveals
Bernardine's theatypical approach:

> The Blessed Virgin could do more concerning God than God
> could do concerning himself ... Now, God came to the
> Virgin, and it was necessary for the Virgin to give birth, and
> to none other than God, and not by any other than God. Now
> God, could only generate God from himself; and yet the
> Virgin made a Man. God could only generate someone
> infinite, immortal, eternal, impassable, impalpable, invisible,
> in the form of God; but the Virgin made him finite, mortal,
> poor, temporal, palpable, sentient, visible, in the form of a
> servant, in a created nature ... O the unthinkable power of
> the Virgin Mother! ...
>
> One Hebrew woman invaded the house of the eternal
> King; one girl, I do not know by what caresses, pledges or
> violence, seduced, deceived and, if I may say so, wounded
> and enraptured the divine heart and ensnared the Wisdom
> of God ... Surely it was quite impossible for God to do such a
> thing by himself.[29]

Here Mary's dominance appears to know no bounds. One
final example from the work of Jean Jacques Olier (d. AD1657) is
worthy of remark. Olier was the founder of the seminary of St
Sulpice in Paris for the purpose of educating priests. His
theatypical approach has a connubial element attaching to it
where he focuses on the symbolic relationship between the
Father and the Blessed Virgin. In this marriage, the possessions
of the husband belong to the wife which means that God has
arranged the salvation of humankind according to Mary's
wishes. He is no longer the First Cause but his will depends on
hers.[30] This is a reference to Aquinas's (AD1224-1274) theology
of God as the First Cause.[31] As well as being the spouse of God,

29. Cited in Graef, *Mary*, Vol 1, pp 316-317
30. Cited in Graef, *Mary*, Vol 2, pp 35-36
31. See Eoin Cassidy, *The Search for Meaning and Values*, Dublin: Veritas,
2004, pp 219-220

Mary is also the spouse of Christ glorified. Olier expresses it thus: 'It seems to me that Jesus and Mary are wholly consummated into one and are but one thing.'[32] It could be read, however, that this statement is not so much about her relationship with Christ but rather about the curtailing of his power and the transference of it to Mary. She possesses powerful omnipotence to do with it as she wishes even if that means binding the power of Christ by preventing the evil he might be tempted to do to the guilty.[33]

Prominence so far has been placed on the *Theotokos* title, claiming that it was the portal through which Mary was elevated well beyond the mortal woman of Nazareth of two thousand years ago. Although the title itself has largely contributed to Mary's excessive exaltation, it did not do so alone. Other important teachings such as her perpetual virginity and motherhood, the dogmatic pronouncement on the Immaculate Conception and her unique relationship with the Holy Spirit were also partially responsible for that exaltation. The following sections will now show that these elements each in their own way are key factors in the advancement of the theatypical approach.

Mary's Virginity: In Partu and Post-Partum

Essentially, Mary's exaltation finds its original roots in the teaching on the virginal conception of Jesus where the scriptures clearly advert to it in the infancy narratives (Mt 1:18-25; Lk 1:26-38). The narratives have held a fascination for Christians throughout the centuries, the pinnacle of which was Mary's incredulous 'Yes' (Lk 1:38) to Gabriel at the annunciation. It was from that moment onwards that the unique phenomenon of 'virginal mother' came into existence. The virginal conception required explanatory doctrines and as the early centuries progressed they were not in short supply from the fathers of the church and successive theologians. Through a series of arguments and counter arguments, the complex doctrine of the meaning of Mary's perpetual virginity and motherhood evolved. The debates often resulted in confusion over the doctrine, making it

32. Cited in Graef, *Mary*, Vol 2, pp 38-39
33. Cited in Graef, *Mary*, Vol 2, p 39

difficult possibly even today for members of the faithful to comprehend fully. A brief summary may, therefore, be of use before proceeding any further. O'Carroll usefully provides the three traditional stages of Mary's perpetual virginity and motherhood: (i) Mary of Nazareth conceived her son Jesus while still remaining a virgin; (ii) this virginity was not altered by childbirth; (iii) in her marriage to Joseph she did not have sexual relations with him. The first stage, that is the virginal conception, appears to be confirmed by the scriptures and is otherwise known as *virginitas ante partum*. The second stage came through church intuition, *virginitas in partu*, and the third stage, the perpetual virginity or *virginitas post partum*, has been advocated by most theologians from early Christian times.[34] These three Latin phrases are explanations of the ancient title *Aeiparthenos* (Ever Virgin).

The early second-century work, the *Protoevangelium of James*, pays special attention to Mary's virginity. Its principal aim was to prove the perpetual virginity of Mary before, during and after the birth of Christ. In the text, a test confirms Mary's virginity before birth and the absence of labour pains coupled with a midwife's examination, demonstrates Mary's virginity during birth.[35] The work, however, as it deals only with the infancy of Jesus, does not explicitly assert Mary's perpetual virginity, that is, her continued virginal state subsequent to the birth of Christ. It cannot be said that there was complete unanimity among the early writers on the matter. Tertullian (c. AD160-220), although he accepted Mary's virginal conception, also claimed that childbirth ended Mary's physical virginity. Thus he denies that Mary was a virgin *in partu* and *post-partum*. The reason, according to John Quasten, is that Tertullian is eager to stress the real humanity of Christ. Since, for Tertullian, Christ's body was not heavenly he had to be born from the usual natural substance of human flesh. Christ was, therefore, born from the very substance of Mary, ex Maria.[36]

Origen (AD185-254), on the other hand, expressly states his belief in the perpetual virginity implying it is a truth already

---

34. O'Carroll, *Theotokos*, p 357
35. Ruether, *Mary – The Feminine Face of the Church*, pp 54-55
36. John Quasten, *Patrology*, Utrecht: Spectrum Publishers, 1966, p 329

recognised as an integral part of the deposit of faith.[37] By the fourth-century Jerome (AD347-420), a renowned exegete and ascetic, also argued in favour of Mary's perpetual virginity but he emphasised it in the belief that virginity was a superior state to marriage. Two churchmen, Helvidius and Jovinian, however, had no intention of accepting the superiority of virginity over marriage, claiming that they were of equal value to the life of the Christian. To strengthen their case against the great Jerome, they used Mary as their example of someone who had conceived as a virgin but subsequently lived the life of a married mother, having been inseminated by Joseph her spouse. This gave extreme offence not only to Jerome but also to Ambrose Bishop of Milan (AD339-397) where he convened a local council (c. AD390) to consider the arguments submitted. The doctrine set fourth at that council categorically defended Mary's perpetual virginity.[38]

The debate nonetheless remains even today, especially with respect to Mary's marriage to Joseph and the scriptural evidence that Jesus had siblings. Anthony Tambasco conveys that much of this ancient controversy centres on Matthew and Mark. Matthew, for his part, implies that after the birth of Jesus, Joseph and Mary had normal marital relations (Mt 1:25). In addition, both Matthew (13:55-56) and Mark (6:3) write about Mary's being the mother of other sons and daughters. They tell of the 'brothers' and 'sisters' of Jesus and give names to some of them.[39] Wilfrid Harrington outlines the customary responses to the controversy of Jesus' brothers and sisters (Mark 6:3) when he writes:

> There are three main views as to what the text means: (1) that they were full blood brothers and sisters of Jesus (Helvidius); (2) that they were children of Joseph by a former wife (Epiphanius); (3) that they were cousins of Jesus (Jerome). For all who accept the perpetual virginity of Mary, the first view is obviously excluded; and the second has very much

37. O'Carroll, *Theotokos*, pp 274-275
38. O'Carroll, *Theotokos*, pp 17-22
39. Anthony Tambasco, *What are they saying about Mary?* New York: Paulist Press, 1984, p 22

the air of an *ad hoc* solution. In favour of the third position is the fact that the term 'brother' regularly has a broader meaning in the Old Testament. And the interpretation is supported by the fact that two of the 'brothers' mentioned here, James and Joses, are elsewhere (15:40) said to be sons of another Mary. Thus, though one's interpretation (these are cousins of Jesus) is prompted by factors outside of Mark, his text can bear that interpretation.[40]

The virginal conception, *in partu and post-partum*, makes breathtaking demands on the Christian believer, for all time defying theological reflection and narrative. This unique and amazing difference between Mary and all other mortal women adds to her mystery, grandeur and wonder leading to palatable and authoritative stories about her purity and imagery. Here we have a woman whose unique birth-giving denies the ordered structure of co-creation as designed by God but nonetheless permitted as it comes only from God. Mary's *in partu and post-partum* speak of one singular exception in the whole of humankind with whom none can be compared.

Mary's Virginal Conception: Ante Partum

Although the *in partu* and *post-partum* debates are important, the bulk of Christian literature has continually concentrated on Mary's *virginitas ante partum*, her virginity before the birth of Jesus. The formidable Raymond Brown has concluded that the scriptures leave the historicity an open question, in claiming that it cannot be decided on scriptural evidence alone.[41] He indicates, in the strict exegesis of the historical critical method, that it cannot be proven because it is not known where Matthew (1:18-21) and Luke (2:1-7) got the idea from as there is no known evidence of, 'an exact parallel … in the material available to Christians' from either Greek mythology or Hellenistic Judaism. He concludes that scientifically we are left with an unresolved problem as to how we deal with the 'very unpleasant alternative' of adulterous conception by Mary during her betrothal to Joseph

---

40. Wilfrid Harrington, *Mark*, Dublin: Veritas, 1979, pp 77-78
41. Raymond Brown, *The Birth of the Messiah*, New York: Image Books, 1977, pp 298-309

which he refers to as the illegitimacy of Jesus.[42] Needless to say Brown may not always have been accepted among some of his peers at times for this particular interpretation, either for going too far or for not going far enough.

Even more disconcerting for some Christians is Jane Schaberg's theory that the virginal conception is perhaps no more than a human fantasy. For her, it is a deeply anti-sexual notion making neither human nor theological sense – an idea which comes from her research into the 'illegitimacy' of Jesus. Schaberg claims that Matthew and Luke intended their readers to understand the illegitimate conception of Jesus as God's option for a wronged and oppressed woman. However, this did not happen through any virginal conception, rather Mary was either seduced or raped, the latter being the more likely case.[43] No doubt for many, Schaberg's interpretation is contentious when she proposes that the conception of Jesus came to pass in such a way. Nonetheless, it does appear to make some sense to Monica Hellwig, who first raised the question among feminist theologians about the conception of Jesus resulting from the rape of his mother.[44] Hellwig was painstaking in her scriptural and theological research, finding the illegitimacy theory doctrinally acceptable. However, she did not follow her thesis through, possibly due to fear of reprisal or lack of conclusive evidence.

Shocking as the claims of the illegitimacy of Jesus and the defiling of Mary are, those who believe this to be likely are re-reading the scriptures from a not altogether abnormal perspective. Gratuitous violence and rape of women were not infrequent at that time. Given the historical and political situation of the day, Mary's victimisation at the hands of a wicked scoundrel would have been fairly commonplace as, indeed, it is today for countless numbers of women in our so-called 'sanitised' western world. In addition, women were second in ranking order to men and their voices in law were weak, if heard at all. Although the illegitimacy

---

42. Raymond Brown, 'The Problem of the Virginal Conception of Jesus', *Theological Studies*, Vol 33, (1972), pp 23-33
43. Jane Schaberg, *The Illegitimacy of Jesus: A Feminist Theological Interpretation of the Infancy Narratives*, San Francisco: Harper and Row, 1987.
44. Monika Hellwig, 'The Dogmatic Implications of the Birth of the Messiah', *Emmanuel*, Vol 84, (1978), pp 21-24

question is not to be found anywhere in official teaching, it may well be inauthentic to ignore the work of scholars whose learned enquiries jolt us into contemplating the human drama of Mary at a much deeper level than we might otherwise be disposed to do. This is not to suggest, however, that two thousand years of tradition expounding the great mysteries about the conception of Jesus the Christ are in any way untrue or invalid for today's theologians, Christians or members of the church.

Regardless of centuries of arguments and counter-arguments, church teaching insists on Mary's perpetual, virginal mother-hood *ante-partum, in-partu* and *post-partum.* The result of this teaching, according to Marina Warner, was to remove her as far as possible from the taint of the sin of humankind. It was a sign of her exceptional purity, her total sinlessness and her utter unquestioning commitment to God. Also it removed Mary from every human being, particularly women, so that those who were devoted to her would of necessity feel their inferiority whenever they contemplated her. As Warner reminisces:

> The virgin, sublime model of chastity, nevertheless remained for me the most holy being I could ever contemplate, and so potent was her spell that for some years I could not enter a church without pain at all the safety and beauty of the salvation I had forsaken.[45]

The real significance overall is that Mary's perpetual virginity is an extraordinary phenomenon, whether one chooses to accept it or not. This 'sublime model of chastity' is quite incredible to the human mind, even when taken in the context of the great religious mysteries of all time. The paradox of Mary as virgin and mother illustrates decisively the very epitome of her glorification and her otherness as a paragon of virtue and chastity. The exemplary personification of Mary's holiness, with its roots in her virginal motherhood, never to be matched by another human being, makes its own contribution to Mary as Theatype.

The Immaculate Conception
Coupled with Mary's status as perpetual virgin and mother was the belief that she was immaculately conceived. In 1854, the title

45. Marina Warner, *Alone of All her Sex*, London: Pan Books, 1976, p XXI

'Immaculate Conception' was proclaimed as a dogma of the church by Pius IX[46] which in its turn contributed greatly to the image of Mary as Theatype. The title was a privilege which ensured that Mary would remain above and beyond normal human experiential understanding. Although the doctrine eventually culminated in an infallible dogmatic pronouncement, it had a long history of dispute. Boss explains that the Franciscan order was among the strongest defenders of the doctrine during the Middle Ages although it continued to be opposed by the Dominicans up until the seventeenth-century.[47] Four years later, in 1858, a beautiful heavenly creature appeared to the child Bernadette at Lourdes in France identifying herself in the words, 'I am the Immaculate Conception', arguably vindicating the dogma to the faithful of the world.[48]

The official pronouncement by Pius IX on Mary as being immaculately conceived came with the following declaration:

> ... the soul of the Blessed Virgin Mary, during her creation and at the moment of its infusion into the body, was enriched with the grace of the Holy Ghost, and was preserved free from original sin ... and of the worship established in honour of the Conception of the same Virgin Mary Mother of God, and rendered to her according to that pious opinion; these we renew, and under the censures and penalties decreed in the same constitutions, we command that they be carried into effect.[49]

This promulgation was the climax of a tormented debate that had begun approximately in the fourth-century with Ephrem (AD306-373) and was endlessly argued by theologians of the church up until the Council of Trent (1545-1563). At this time also, Trent explicitly refused to include Mary in its decree on

46. Pius IX., 'Apostolic Constitution of Pope Pius IX on the Immaculate Conception (December 8, 1854)' [online] http://www.newadvent. org/library/docs_pi09id.htm [Accessed 5 February 2008]
47. Sarah Boss, 'The Development of the Doctrine of Mary's Immaculate Conception' in S. Boss (ed), Mary the Complete Resource, New York: Oxford University Press, 2007, p 207
48. Ruth Harris, Lourdes: Body and the Spirit in the Secular Age, London: Penguin, 1999, pp. 357-358
49. Ulick Bourke, The Bull 'Ineffabilis', Dublin: J. Mullaney, 1868, pp 28-29

original sin. O'Carroll recounts the history subsequent to that council which led to further papal interventions on the matter. He writes:

> ... between 1600 and 1800 the Jesuits alone brought out 300 works on the Immaculate Conception ... On December 1667, a landmark was reached. Pope Alexander VII issued the bull *Sollicitudo omnium Ecclesiarum* ... On 15 May 1695, Innocent XII imposed on the whole church the Office and Mass of the Immaculate Conception, with Octave; on 6 December 1708, Clement XI established the feast as a holyday of obligation ... {Pius IX} ... first made a consultation of the entire hierarchy of the church {*Ubi primum*, 2 February 1849} and found it practically unanimous on the subject. Then he set cardinals and theologians to work on the composition of an appropriate text ... It was not an age of critical scholarship ... there were practically no footnotes, few references to fathers ... the essential words 'preserved free from stain of original sin' were written into the Constitution on the Church [and then] published by Vatican II (*LG* 59).[50]

A brief reference to the meaning of original sin in the context of the Immaculate Conception is necessary at this juncture. Although the term 'original sin' is not a biblical one, Paul's text to the Romans (Rom 5:12) has been interpreted as a source of the doctrine. Denis Carroll explains his account of the teaching by describing three possible meanings. Firstly, that Adam as the first human being influences the rest of humanity by his bad example. Secondly, Adam's sin leaves us with an inherited tendency to sin through human weakness. Thirdly, Adam makes us all sinners whether or not we wish to be. The third interpretation is the traditional one.[51]

The importance of Carroll's explanation is evident in the light of the dogma of the Immaculate Conception promulgated to eliminate even the slightest possibility of Mary being tainted

---

50. Michael O'Carroll,'The Immaculate Conception and Assumption of Our Lady in Today's Thinking' in J. Hyland (ed), *Mary in the Church*, Dublin: Veritas, 1989, pp 48-49
51. Denis Carroll, *Towards a Story of the Earth*, Dublin: Dominican Publications, 1987, pp 89-117

by original sin. Mary soars above the rest of humankind so that not even for the briefest moment of her existence had she experienced this privation. From the instant her soul was created and united to her body, she received sanctifying grace – a special status assigned to Mary setting her uniquely apart from all other human beings.[52]

Boff: Mary as Theatype

The Immaculate Conception title bestowed on Mary is a doctrinal theology with a supernatural emphasis, somewhat overshadowing Mary's natural womanhood and largely contributing to her image as the great exception. Certainly it can be argued in present day terms that this doctrine contributed to Mary as Theatype if one considers the work of the Latin American theologian Leonardo Boff. Central to Boff's thesis is his understanding of the relationship between the Immaculate Conception and the virginal motherhood. Boff maintains that the Immaculate Conception of the Virgin Mary contains a secret meaning. Through Mary's Immaculate Conception, God has begun to create a new humanity free from all sin. Here is a perfectly pure woman who has been prepared by God as a receptacle for God's own sinless Son. As Boff expresses it:

> In her, the feminine, charged with divinity, reaches its fullness. Still a virgin, she becomes a mother, and conceives God the Son. The secret, ultimate meaning of the Immaculate Conception lies not in Mary, but in God's wish to become incarnate. God determines to communicate the divine self totally. God prepares a living temple as dwelling place. God enters it, assumes it, *and renders it divine* (emphasis added). This preparation for the future spiritualisation of humanity is the meaning and scope of the Immaculate Conception.[53]

Here Boff is emphasising that the Son of God could not have dwelt in any receptacle that was tainted by sin but, in doing so, he claims that Mary's womb is the temple which God renders 'divine'. Mary's Immaculate Conception is more than just a

52. Canice Maloney, *Mary*, Dublin: Gill and Son, 1936, pp 52-53
53. Leonardo Boff, *The Maternal Face of God*, London: Collins, 1987, pp 132-133

particular view of the necessity of her sinlessness. She is the culmination of humanity and the coronation of Israel as Boff poetically ponders, '(at) long last, a creature has appeared in the universe who is pure goodness. Now the desert blooms, now the tree of life produces flowers that do not wither before summer.'[54] In that same context, Boff upholds the perpetual virginity of Mary as it is taught in the tradition because he sees it as the seed of divinised humanity.[55]

Mary's participation in the divine activity allowed the eternal God to become 'linked to all of humanity by way of an umbilical cord'.[56] Boff introduces a novel reason for emphasising the virginity of Mary and her divine motherhood. Here is where Boff's approach reaches theatypical zenith when he states that, '(the) Spirit dwelt within her, assumed her, and lifted her to the level of divinity'.[57] Furthermore, Mary engendered a human being who is also God. She engendered the true God through her relationship in union with the Holy Spirit. In Boff's mind, there is a clear relationship between the divinisation of Mary and the divinisation of the fruit of her womb, Jesus. Developing this train of thought, he goes on to say that the, 'flesh that Mary has bestowed on Jesus is the flesh of God. Accordingly, something of Mary's femininity has been hypostatically assumed by God.'[58] This gives the feminine an eternal dimension so that, 'in Jesus the feminine is God' ... and ... '[in] Jesus the feminine has been divinised'.[59]

Once Boff has hold of the reins he keeps going. By a complex yet determined system of argumentation he claims that, 'God can divinise the feminine, as the divine Persons are capable of

54. Boff, *The Maternal Face of God*, pp 128-131
55. See Boff, *The Maternal Face of God*, p 136. Boff also believes that the Incarnation of God was not necessarily bound to a virginal conception. God could just as readily have engendered someone through human love to be the incarnation of his Son. God incarnate in this way would not have been any less the Saviour or any less the Son of God. Nonetheless, Boff chooses not to accept the conception of Jesus on normal biological grounds
56. Boff, *The Maternal Face of God*, p 158
57. Boff, *The Maternal Face of God*, p 158
58. Boff, *The Maternal Face of God*, p 78
59. Boff, *The Maternal Face of God*, p 89

hypostatically assuming a concrete human nature, and human nature has the obediential potency to be so assumed.'[60] In Boff's questionable theology, he believes that Mary not only received the effects of the Holy Spirit in her life (as everyone has) 'but that she specifically received the very person and godhead of the Third Person of the Holy Trinity.'[61] He then follows with the shocking statement, 'Mary is raised to the level of God in order to be able to engender God. Only the divine can engender the divine … Mary is assumed by the Holy Spirit, and thus elevated to the level of God.'[62]

Hans Urs von Balthasar has difficulty with Mary's attainment of this level of divinity in the work of Boff. Breandán Leahy, commenting on Balthasar, explains:

> No matter how much he links the Spirit with Mary at the annunciation, however, Von Balthasar is careful not to fall into a false exaggeration. Commenting on L. Boff's mariology, he praises much of it that is beautiful and in agreement with tradition but questions his contention that Mary was overshadowed by the Holy Spirit in such a way that she can and must be described as hypostatically united with the Spirit.[63]

Boff has his reasons for this controversial elevation of Mary. Firstly, he is influenced by fellow Franciscan Maximilian Kolbe who traded his life for the freedom of another prisoner at Auschwitz during World War II. Kolbe describes Mary in terms of her relationship with the Holy Trinity. She is the one created person in whom we best recognise and find reflected the Holy Trinity through a spousal connection. Secondly, Boff is a

---

60. Boff, *The Maternal Face of God*, pp 94-95
61. Boff, *The Maternal Face of God*, p 97
62. Boff, *The Maternal Face of God*, p 101. Boff was told to submit for censorship any theological writings he wished to publish. He was not permitted to make public statements and he was ordered to abstain from preaching, teaching and writing. However, this directive came as a result of his criticism of certain church structures but not for his teachings on the relationship between Mary and the Holy Spirit. See Leonardo Boff, *Church, Charism and Power*, New York: The Crossroad Publishing Company, 1981.
63. Brendan Leahy, *The Marian Profile*, London: New City, 2000, p 83

Brazilian liberation theologian who has been embroiled in the
hot-bed of political intrigue and strife in a country teeming with
poor and oppressed people. Like so many more in Latin
America, he has walked in fear of his life. Therefore, he is
acutely aware of the plight of women in that situation in
particular whom he knows to be doubly oppressed because of
their sexuality. Boff's hope is to reassure such women that they
do, indeed, have direct access to the Spirit and it is essential that
they also see themselves reflected in some way in the divine. If
Mary is raised above everyone, particularly through her
hypostatisation in the Holy Spirit, then she is the feminine face
of God. In this way, Boff seeks sexual reciprocity for women in
the divine from a tradition which has so often rebuffed them. He
explains:

> The Spirit, the eternal feminine, is united to the created
> feminine in order that the latter may be totally and fully
> what it can be – virgin and mother. Mary, as Christian piety
> has always intuited, is the eschatological realisation of the
> feminine in all of its dimensions.[64]

Yet Boff's desire to include female reciprocity for women in
the divine through Mary, according to Elizabeth Johnson, is
illogical. She points out, '... even Boff's analysis of the feminine
in relation to the Virgin Mary runs aground, finally, on the rocks
of inconsistency'.[65] The inconsistency is born out of his attend-
ance to Jungian psychology and his lack of criticism of it where
Jung equates the feminine with, 'dark, death, depth, and
receptivity and the masculine with light, transcendence, outgoing-
ness, and reason ... coupled with his limitation of this feminine
dimension to the Spirit alone within the godhead, insures an
outcome that is not liberating for women'.[66]

Johnson then is unwilling to progress along the path of Mary
as the feminine face of God for two reasons. Firstly, it will have
implications for the Third Person of the Trinity who is likely to
end up as an amorphous female – an unsatisfactory situation

---

64. Boff, *The Maternal Face of God*, p 101
65. Elizabeth Johnson, *She Who Is: The Mystery of God in Feminist
Theological Discourse*, New York: Crossroad, 1993, p 52
66. Johnson, *She Who Is*, pp 52-53

which portrays the Father and the Son as much stronger images than the Spirit. The Spirit, in this sense, is a weak principle as the feminine face of the godhead. Secondly, despite the good will of Boff's intent for women they cannot be, 'equated exclusively with mothering, affectivity, darkness, virginity ... without suffocating women's potential'.[67] Instead, Johnson holds that in order to portray the mystery of the Trinity in a more attractive way, Mary must simply be reflective of the female face of God so that Marian theology and its attendant devotion have a part to play in, 'the crucial task of imaging God in inclusive fashion'.[68] Her intention, therefore, is to mine the Marian tradition for the purposes of retrieving female imagery by focusing on images of God other than male. Such images include Mary's revelation of divine love, closeness, interest and trustworthiness of human-kind. This, Johnson says, is an acceptable theology on the grounds that these symbols function to reveal the divine love as always ready to hear and respond to human needs. In this way, Mary is not likely to be imaged as part of the godhead.[69] Rather what is required is a theology which brings out female aspects of the divine in the Trinity, but imaging Mary as the female element is not the answer.[70]

The Spirit and Mary

The deficiency of female images of God in the tradition and the attempt to find a place for them in Mary through the Spirit is also noted by Maria Bingemer. She claims that the church has neglected pneumatology. At times, language used in the scriptures to describe the Holy Spirit (the Paraclete) such as intercessor, helper, advocate, defender, consoler and counsellor was transferred to Mary (Jn 14:16; 15:26; 16:7).[71] In this respect, it can certainly be argued that the transference of these titles from

---

67. Johnson, *She Who Is*, pp 53-54

68. Elizabeth Johnson, 'Mary and the Female Face of God', *Theological Studies*, Vol 50, (1989), p 501

69. Johnson, 'Mary and the Female Face of God', pp 500-526

70. Ruether, *Mary – The Feminine Face of the Church*, pp 34-56. See also Sally McFague, *Models of God*, London: SCM Press, 1987

71. Maria Bingemer, 'Women: Time and Eternity the Eternal Woman and the Feminine Face of God', *Concilium*, Vol 6, (1991), pp 98-107

the Spirit to Mary contributed effectively to the imaging of Mary as Theatype. Peculiarly for those such as Spretnak, the replacement of the Spirit by Mary does not go far enough. Indeed, she even believes that Mary's role has been usurped by the Spirit, evident from the following quotation, 'In the modernised church, the Holy Spirit is now situated in (triumphant) competition with Mary, invoked to trump her at every possible opportunity.'[72] Spretnak embellishes her concern about the Spirit usurping Mary's role upon her receipt of a present of a set of rosary beads from Rome. Her reaction to the gift is worth quoting as a testimony to the strength of her feelings:

> I held the silver beads in my hands, marvelling at the beauty of the details. Suddenly I noticed something strange and felt a tightening in my solar plexus. At the spot where an image of Mary is always found, she was not there. I stared in disbelief. There was something odd in her place, some sort of logo ... of swirling flames? Eventually I perceived that the design was a circle of four stylised, swirling doves: the symbol of the Holy Spirit. Banishing Mary even from the rosary? Could this be? Using the Holy Spirit to displace her? Could the'modernisers' actually have gone this far?[73]

Indeed, far from banishing Mary from the rosary, the image of Mary as Theatype in relation to the Holy Spirit is evident where Boff and Spretnak are concerned. It must be stated that theology of this nature is, by and large, likely to be unacceptable to many theologians. Kari Borresen, for example, would not countenance imaging Mary beyond that which she has received through recognised tradition. She expresses exaggerated aberrations as anathema describing the 'divinisation' of Mary as, 'a noxious deviation which could otherwise be termed as heretical'.[74] Nonetheless, disturbing as the above accounts of the relationship between Mary and the Holy Spirit might be for those who do not image Mary as Theatype, the fact remains that

---

72. Spretnak, *Missing Mary*, p 57
73. Spretnak, *Missing Mary*, p 57
74. Kari Borresen, 'Mary in Catholic Theology', *Concilium*, Vol 168, (1983), p 50

there is certain evidence to sustain the claim that the theatypical approach is alive and well in some of today's theologians.

Conclusion

In conclusion to this chapter, we have seen examples of an accumulation of excerpts from the early fathers of the church and from ancient and modern theologians with respect to mariology in the Christian tradition. Although some of the early theologians were not men of great significance, others brought to bear considerable influence over entire generations of Christians. In this respect, we gleaned insights into an ever increasing practice of elevating Mary beyond the bounds acceptable to the tradition. It could even be said that among its numbers the respective populace of each generation came dangerously close to displacing God through virtual worship of Mary. This sometimes habitual practice of 'deification', intentional or otherwise, began with various interpretations of the scriptures and doctrinal statements such as Mary's virginal conception, perpetual virginity, the title *Theotokos*, reaching its crescendo in the Middle Ages and culminating in her 'hypostatic' relationship with the Holy Spirit. It might even be argued that a goddess-starved faithful have been responsible for the emergence of Mary as Theatype, as she has been described above.

Today Mary is ubiquitous in many parts of the world through her shrines, churches and grottos. Can every Catholic truly say that he or she, in the darkest of hours, have less confidence of a positive outcome when petitioning Mary than when petitioning God? Certainly, there are innumerable counter-arguments to claim that the phenomenon of Mary as Theatype ever existed, but given the evidence, particularly from the Middle Ages until today, total denial would be difficult to sustain. Even church teaching itself was at times ambiguous about Mary's role. As James Mackey expresses it, 'What, then, is the status of Mary in the public theology and doctrine of the Roman Catholic Church? Always flirting with the divinity of Mary, I should be inclined to answer, but always finally, officially and loudly denying it.'[75] As to where Mary will reach

75. James Mackey, 'The use and abuse of Mary in Roman Catholicism' in Holloway (ed), *Who Needs Feminism?* London: SPCK, 1991, pp 99-116

in times to come in the aftermath of the so-called post Vatican II 'dogmatic slumber'[76] only God (or perhaps Mary) can tell?

---

76. The term 'dogmatic slumber' is used by Spretnak to describe a belief in the neglect of Mary subsequent to the Second Vatican Council. Spretnak, *Missing Mary*, p 108

CHAPTER TWO

They called her Christ?

She claims no crown from Christ apart, who gave God life and limb,
She only claims a broken heart because of him.[1]

Mary as Christatype

Mary as Christatype brings into focus the second category of the
three broad Marian types under discussion.[2] The essence of
imaging Mary in this way is that it places her almost on a par
with Christ as the perfect example of human existence. The basis
of the christatypical approach emerged among the populace,
possibly as a consequence of theological debate initiated by the
early fathers and certain other theologians during the first four-
hundred years of Christianity. At that early stage, Mary was not
at the heart of Christian teaching, nor was her role in relation to
Christ particularly well developed. Theological uncertainty
often abounded, leading to ambiguous statements about her,
which placed Mary in a position very close to Christ while also
admitting of her human frailties. Marian frailties were not
reflected in the titles and privileges later promulgated by the
church. Although Mary was never officially intended to be the
focus of any doctrines which pertain solely to Christ, as
devotion to her traversed the centuries, certain christological
interpretations accrued around her *persona,* exaggerating the role
she played in the mystery of redemption.

Imaging Mary as Christatype departs substantially from that
of mainstream Catholic Christian teaching. For example, the
Constitution on the Liturgy, as it is found in the documents of
the Second Vatican Council, clearly teaches that Mary 'is
inseparably linked with her son's saving work. In her the church

1. Anketell Kennedy,'Good Friday Falls on Lady Day', p 98
2. This is not to be confused with term *'Christotypical'* a phrase used by
some theologians to describe Mary's unique role at her Son's side in his
work of salvation. See Elizabeth Johnson, *Truly our Sister*, New York:
Continuum, (2003), p 129

admires and exalts the most excellent fruit of redemption, and joyfully contemplates, as in a faultless image, that which she herself desires and hopes wholly to be.'[3] Clearly official Marian titles which associate Mary with Christ such as Co-Redeemer and Mediatrix were never intended to contribute to any form of distortion nor were they promulgated to permit the usurpation of Christ by Mary. However, it is not difficult to see how mariological misinterpretations sometimes came about as a result of the complex theological doctrines pertaining to Christ. Add to this the Dogma of the Assumption, include the apparitions' phenomena, and we have the ingredients that constitute the christatypical approach.

The Christatype Emerging

Mary was not the primary concern of ancient Christian writers. Rather they wished to protect their emerging doctrines from unwelcome and potentially harmful pagan or heretical influence. In reference to this difficult pre-Nicene period (prior to AD325), Tina Beattie explains:

> Ante-Nicene theology took shape in a turbulent era when Christianity was a minority religion spread across the Roman Empire, representing a plurality of beliefs and devotions in different geographical and cultural contexts, with many of its followers being subjected to persecution and martyrdom. Early Christian doctrine was clarified through being challenged and defended in intense intellectual debates and cultural and political conflicts.[4]

Furthermore, the early fathers had to contend with their own internal theological squabbles. Beattie continues:

> Some of the church fathers, such as Justin Martyr (100/100-65), Clement of Alexandria (d. 215) and his successor in the Alexandrian School, Origen (185-254), sought to emphasise the compatibilities between Christianity and Greek thought,

---

3. Vatican Council II, *The Counciliar and Post Counciliar Documents, Sacrosanctum concilium* in A. Flannery (ed), Dublin: Dominican Publications, 1975, par 103
4. Tina Beattie, 'Mary in Patristic Theology' in S. Boss (ed), *Mary the Complete Resource*, New York: Oxford University Press, 2007, p 75

while others such as Tertullian (c.160-post-220) were vehemently opposed to such accommodations. Tertullian famously asked, 'What then do Athens and Jerusalem have to do with one another?' Henry Chadwick suggests that 'he proposes that the correct and indeed the only true answer to his questions is "Nothing whatsoever".'[5]

In addition, the scarcity of references to Mary in the scriptures compounded by, as yet, an undeveloped Marian theology led to considerable ambiguity among the fathers as to her role and function in their teachings. Irenaeus, Bishop of Lyons (d. c. AD200), for example, like many of his contemporaries finds himself having to respond to rampant and troublesome heresies such as Gnosticism. Unfortunately, but not untypical of the fathers, Irenaeus' deliberations for the cause of righteousness in Christianity resulted in denigration of women, perhaps not altogether intentional. In these instances, he praises Mary's goodness and obedience over against Eve's disobedience, where the latter was to be held forever responsible in Christianity for spiralling humankind into bondage and separation from God. This was not just a simple contrast between Eve and Mary. Rather Irenaeus was emphasising how Mary's obedience to the will of God was tied up with her divine motherhood and her intercessory role in the mystery of redemption. Mary's obedient will, her divine motherhood and her intercessory role are expressed by Irenaeus in the following way:

> Mary the Virgin is found obedient, saying: Behold the handmaid of the Lord ... Eve, however, disobedient: for she did not obey, even though she was still a virgin. Inasmuch as she, having indeed Adam for a husband, yet being still a virgin, became disobedient and was made both for herself and the whole human race the cause of death, so also Mary, having a husband destined for her yet being a virgin, by obeying, became the cause of salvation both for herself and the whole human race ... Thus also was the knot of Eve's disobedience dissolved by Mary's obedience; for what the

---

5. Beattie, 'Mary in Patristic Theology', pp 75-76
6. Cited in Graef, *A History of Doctrine and Devotion*, Vol 1, p 39

virgin Eve had tied up by unbelief, this the Virgin Mary loosened by faith.[6]

Irenaeus was referring to Mary as the New Eve, no doubt paralleling the idea to Christ as the New Adam, where the basis for the latter is found in Paul's Fourth Letter to the Romans (5:12-21). Mary's obedient status, for Irenaeus, is clearly far above that of the sinful Eve, as her intercessory role begins to show itself in salvation history by association with the mystery of redemption. Ambiguously, however, Mary's human frailty and imperfection as yet coexist in Irenaeus. In his exegesis of the marriage feast of Cana (Jn 2:1-12), for example, he interprets Jesus' rather abrupt response to his mother, 'You must not tell me what to do ... my time has not yet come' (Jn 2:4) as, 'the Lord *repels* her untimely haste'.[7] Despite the significance that Irenaeus holds for Mary in the mystery of redemption, he has no hesitation in admitting of her weakness and lack of comprehension of the first great miracle accounted for in the gospel of John. Since Irenaeus expects obedience of the faithful if they are to be saved, he infuses Mary into the salvific process by contrasting her with the disobedient Eve, but nonetheless capable of misunderstanding her Son's mission.

Tertullian (AD160-220), although not one of the early fathers, was a theologian of some influence. In his particular tangle with heresy, he plays his own part in the elevation of Mary by contrasting her also with Eve in his deliberations. Like Irenaeus, this is taken at the expense of all other women. Tertullian's perception of their sinfulness is found in excerpts such as, 'What the one had done wrong by believing, the other made good by believing ... Eve ... finally brought forth the diabolic murderer of his brother. Mary, on the contrary, brought forth him who was to redeem Israel, his brother according to the flesh, who had killed him'.[8] Tertullian's unsavoury comment about Eve, the symbolic progenitor of all women, shows to what extent he was prepared to elevate Mary in order to ward off the perplexing heresies he found himself having to contend with. However, his

---

7. Cited in Graef, *A History of Doctrine and Devotion*, Vol 1, p 40 (emphasis added in text above)

8. Cited in Graef, *A History of Doctrine and Devotion*, Vol 1, p 41

understanding of her in relation to Christ is paradoxically witnessed in his exposition of her frailties.

According to Quasten, Tertullian was more concerned with the heresies of his day than he was to make statements about Mary and her relationship with Christ. Tertullian's heretics included the Marcionites, the Basilides and Valentinus all of whom preached some form of gnosticism in an attempt to revive docetism – a heresy which deemed that Christ's body and his crucifixion were an illusion.[9] Evidence of Tertullian's paradox is also recognisable in his interpretation of the scriptures where Jesus sends his mother and brothers away (Mt 12:46 ff) as well as in the dialogue with the woman in the crowd who called out to him, 'Blessed is the womb that bore you' (Lk 11:27). Tertullian claims of these passages that Mary was not one of her Son's followers. In this regard, he even goes so far as to compare her with the unbelieving synagogue insisting that Christ rejected her and, 'transferred the blessedness from the womb and breasts of his mother to his disciples'.[10]

The ambiguities surrounding Mary and her relationship with Jesus are sourced as well in Origen (AD185-254). He boasted of Mary's personal perfection raising her above all other mortals, on the one hand, because of the coming of the Holy Spirit upon her and her divine child-bearing (Lk 1:35). Yet, on the other hand, he implies that Mary's question on this occasion, 'I am a virgin. How, then, can this be?' (Lk 1:34), betrays certain incredulity.[11] Furthermore, and perhaps most telling of Mary's human weakness, was Origen's reference to the Sword of Simeon passage (Lk 2:35) reflecting the relationship between Mary and her Son:

What! Are we to suppose that, when the apostles were scandalised, the Lord's Mother was exempt from scandal? If she did not suffer scandal in the Lord's Passion, Jesus did not

9. Quasten, *Patrology*, pp 282-283. Marcion affirmed Jesus Christ as the saviour sent by God but he rejected the Hebrew Bible and Yahweh; the Basilides claimed to possess a secret tradition handed down from St Peter and St Matthias; Valentinus broke with the church and developed a gnostic doctrine when his efforts to become a bishop failed.
10. Cited in Graef, *A History of Doctrine and Devotion*, Vol 1, pp 43-44
11. Cited in O'Carroll, *Theotokos*, p 274

die for her sins ... even thee shall the sword of unbelief
pierce, and thou shalt be struck with the spear of doubt, and
thy thoughts shall tear thee asunder ... when thou shalt see
him whom thou hadst heard to be the Son of God, and knew
to have been begotten by no seed of man, crucified and
dying, and subject to human torments, and at last with tears
complaining and saying, 'Father, if it be possible, let this
chalice pass from me.'[12]

In this passage, Origen implies that Mary was embarrassed
by the scandal of the circumstance of her Son's death. Furthermore, her imperfections were such that she must have done
wrong, for Jesus had to die for his mother's sins in the same way
that he had to die for everyone else's. Clearly Origen's mind was
fraught with theological quandaries, for as well as having
conceived the Saviour of the world this was coupled with her
humble, painful human circumstance and her need for salvation
at the hands of her Son. Yet despite Origen's, Irenaeus' and
Tertullian's inconsistencies of Mary's imperfections, they laid
the foundation for emulation of her through close association
with her Son. The seeds of her spiritual motherhood, her mysticism
and the uniqueness of her virginal-motherhood status are now
becoming more apparent to us.

The ideal portrayal of Mary as the completely virtuous
Mother of Christ is found in Ambrose (AD339-397). As with
Irenaeus, she is the New Eve who defeated the power of the
devil. She is the woman of incredible strength who is all alone
when the power of the Most High overshadows her. Only the
most special things happen to people when they are alone,
according to Ambrose. The following phrase reveals that a
christatypical understanding of Mary is now coming into its
own: 'She was alone and she worked the redemption of the
world and conceived the redemption of all men.'[13] Pride of place
goes to Mary's virginity when he makes the link between her
virginity, Christ and salvation:

A virgin begot the salvation of the world, a virgin brought

---

12. Cited in O'Carroll, *Theotokos*, p 275
13. Ambrose, 'Letters to Bishops' in Deferrari (ed), *Fathers* 26, Washington
DC: The Catholic University of America Press, 1967, pp 134-135

forth the life of all. Should virginity, then, be abandoned which was of benefit to all in Christ? A virgin carried him whom this world cannot contain or support. And when he is born of Mary's womb, he yet preserved the enclosure of her modesty, and the inviolate seal of her virginity. Thus Christ found in the virgin that which he wanted to be his own, that which the Lord of all might take for himself.[14]

Not only is the christatypical approach evident in the association between Mary's virginity and Christ's salvation, but Ambrose tells of her other almost superhuman qualities at Calvary. As she stood at the cross, Ambrose has it that she did not show any emotion, she did not cry but held fast as men all around her fled the scene. She was not afraid of her Son's slayers but instead offered herself to his persecutors. Ambrose adds to this her spiritual purity which he mentions sixteen times in his writings. Then without denying her genuine humanity, he speaks of Mary as not from this earth but from heaven.[15] Ambrose's recognition of Mary's humanity, while at the same time referring to her as a heavenly creature, is reminiscent of Chalcedon's (AD451) solidification of the orthodox view of its teaching on the dual nature of Jesus.[16]

The Christatype Developing
By the early tenth-century, Mary as Christatype emerges more keenly. The Patriarch of Constantinople Euthymius (d. AD917) and Confessor to the emperor Leo VI (AD866–912) began attributing certain actions to Mary that more fully belong to Christ. In a homily on the conception of St Anne (Mary's mother), he refers to Mary as, 'the royal throne, the incomprehensible ark who will destroy the sanctuaries of the idols and the irrational sacrifices of the Hebrews, who will manifest the great and hidden mystery'.[17] Here he applies to Mary what is said of Christ in Ephesians (2:14-18) when he exhorts, 'she will call back our forefathers and every just soul

---

14. Ambrose, 'Letters to Priests' in Deferrari (ed), *Fathers* 26, Washington DC: The Catholic University of America Press, 1967, pp 332-333
15. O'Carroll, *Theotokos*, p 19
16. See Lane, *The Reality of Jesus*, pp 104-108
17. Cited in Graef, *A History of Doctrine and Devotion*, Vol. 1, pp 195-196

from Hades ... who will sanctify the world ... and destroy all
heresies ...', for the relic of her girdle is brighter then the sun's
rays and more powerful than the heavens.[18]

Christatypical elements attributed to Mary are found also
between the twelfth and the fifteenth centuries. During that
period, Christ becomes ever more removed from humankind
with Mary taking his place as the new symbol of salvation.
According to Rosemary Ruether:

> Teachings about Mary develop as parallels to doctrines
> about Christ and indicate that Mary is a new symbolic figure
> who provides the redemption of humanity. Christ thus
> comes to be seen primarily as the representative of God, and
> so no longer really represents humanity. Mary takes his
> place as the symbol of hope of the human race for final
> salvation.[19]

The development of the christatypical approach to Mary was
partly in reaction to the removal of Christ's human image from
him. In an attempt to provoke the faithful into unquestioning
obedience, Christ was portrayed increasingly as the stern,
authoritarian terrifying figure of the Last Judgement. These
stark images of the Saviour of the world coincided with one of
the darkest times in human history. The Black Death was one of
the deadliest pandemics of all time, peaking in Europe between
1347 and 1351. The total number of mortalities is estimated at 75
million people in the known world, with approximately 25-50
million having occurred in Europe. As medieval thought
progressed, even Christ the *crucified* one was now to become
symbolic of the punishment and judgement of sinners. The
greater the fear of Christ, the greater the trust placed in Mary.[20]
As Ruether explains, 'The paradox of the just and merciful God
is dissolved into the divine wrath, represented by the man Jesus,
as against human mercy represented by the woman Mary.'[21]
Mary becomes evermore the approachable mother who understands the inadequacies of her children and makes allowances

---

18. Cited in Graef, *A History of Doctrine and Devotion*, Vol 1, p 196
19. Ruether, *Mary- The Feminine Face of the Church*, p 62.
20. Ruether, *Mary- The Feminine Face of the Church*, p 64.
21. Ruether, *Mary - The Feminine Face of the Church*, p 62

for them. The more Christ is feared, the more likely the faithful are to transfer their hope, trust and confidence to her for, regardless of their sins, she guarantees the better opportunity of salvation.[22] In this respect, the christatypical approach is one where the faithful recognise Christ's *alter ego* in Mary. She assumes a facet of his personhood, often portraying his human face and sometimes even doing the divine work that would normally be considered his business alone.

Thus devotion to Mary grew over the centuries, where she increasingly took the place of Christ in so many diverse ways. She was feminine and warm, he was masculine and cold. Tears would touch her soul and heartbreak was her bread and butter. Nowhere is this more evident than in the apparitions. Down through the centuries many hundreds of apparitions of Mary have been reported.[23] Mary took the trouble to appear to the poor, to the humble and to the downtrodden – she was tangible where Christ was not. If visionaries and those who witnessed apparitions could see Mary, then she was the portal through which they might reach Christ if and when they needed him.[24] When they flock to her shrines, she is the Christatype.

The Apparitions

Shrines to Mary are well known, but where are those dedicated to her Son (not withstanding his presence in the world's tabernacles)? According to Spretnak, if she has calculated correctly and this is open to question, sixty-six per cent of all Catholic shrines in Europe are established in honour of Mary while only seven per cent are dedicated to Jesus.[25] Through her manifestations to a select few, who in turn passed on her messages to the wider faith community, it could be said that Mary was the source of tangibility that Christ was not. Nothing has quelled the relating of the apparitions of Mary, not even scorn poured forth today as vestiges of earlier, ignorant

---

22. Ruether, *Mary - The Feminine Face of the Church*, p 64
23. See Karl Rahner, *Visions and Prophecies*, London: Burns and Oates, 1963
24. See Richard Rutt, 'Why should he send his Mother? Some theological reflections on Marian apparitions' in W. McLoughlin and J. Pennock (eds), *Mary is for Everyone*, Herefordshire: Gracewing Fowler Wright Books, 1997, pp 276-278. Rutt distinguishes between apparitions and visions.
25. Spretnak, *Missing Mary*, p 105

generations. Such phenomena continue still in our scientific and materialistic world. In the words of Chris Maunder:

> Despite the end of the Cold War by 1991, the apocalyptic strain in Marian apparitions has continued into the twenty-first century. They express a deep unease about the state of the world, its perceived immorality and lack of spirituality which, it is claimed, are leading humanity to disaster. Yet, for the visionaries and their devotees, God wishes to intervene, through Mary, to remedy the situation on our behalf.[26]

The apparitions are difficult either to accept or dispute. Church teaching, for its part, holds its reserve about apparitions and treats them more as permissible pastoral and prayerful experiences rather than as doctrinal or dogmatic directives to the faithful. Nor do they convey new truths but stress Christian virtues rather than the faith of the church. Richard Rutt deliberates on the church's practice of dealing with apparitions when he reminds us that the authentication of apparitions is the business of the local bishops, wherein the Holy See does not take responsibility for them.[27]

In order for an apparition to be authenticated, a bishop must approve it, ensuring that the story does not harm the faith or morals of the Christian community at large. Although after thorough investigation the bishop judges that the event is supernatural, the faithful are not and have never been obliged to believe that such an event ever occurred. Rutt explains: 'Even under the old canons, the church was effectively showing pastoral care rather than making a historical or doctrinal statement'[28] in its treatment of the apparitions. In addition, René Laurentin and René Lejeune, leading authorities on such Marian phenomena, write: 'The church is very prudent with regard to apparitions, and accords them a low status because they are signs which reach us through our senses and are subject to the illusions of subjectivity.'[29]

26. Chris Maunder, 'Apparitions of Mary' in S. Boss (ed), *Mary the Complete Resource*, New York: Oxford University Press, 2007, p 428
27. Rutt, 'Why should he send his Mother?' pp 274-275
28. Rutt, 'Why should he send his Mother?' p 275
29. René Laurentin and René Lejeune, *Messages and Teachings of Mary at Medjugorje*, Ohio: Riehle Foundation, 1988, p 15

Nonetheless, the apparitions are always a vehicle for God's messages to be told through Mary – at least this is held to be the case by countless numbers of Catholic Christians throughout the centuries and today. Mary is God's emissary bearing Christ's message. She does not perform miracles herself, rather she is given permission to be the conduit of them which she receives directly and only from God. Mary is sent; she does not come of her own accord as her will is subject to that of God's. Rather, she opens doors to the mind of God when she is permitted to do so. In this matter, Rahner refers to the opening of 'little doors'[30] which sometimes permits glimpses of the Almighty. Mary's apparitions cannot stand alone and they are not ends in themselves, instead they ask the faithful to be penitent, prayerful and do pilgrimage. When Mary appears as a messenger from God to deliver Christ's message on this earth, she is imaged as the Christatype.

The Apparitions and Popular Piety

Given the phenomena of the apparitions, coupled with the sincerity, devotion and sometimes uncontrolled exuberance of those who believe in their existence, it is difficult to claim that they are not without considerable import to the image of Mary as Christatype. It would be almost impossible to account for the hundreds or more of apparitions, devotional practices, private and communal, that have been reported as having taken place throughout the centuries. Yet, there is a constant increase each year in the numbers of pilgrims who visit the great Marian shrines of the world in their millions. Out of the Marian apparitions reported, a limited few have been given official ecclesiastical approval. The question of approval is very complex and ongoing. Some of those which have been endorsed include Guadalupe, Mexico (1531) to Juan Diego; Paris, France (1830) to Catherine Labouré; La Salette, France (1846) to Maximin Giraud and Melanie Calvat; Lourdes (1858) to Bernadette Soubirous; the Bohemian village of Philippsdorf (1866) to Magdalena Kade; appearances were also reported at Pontmain, Brittany (1871); Pompeii, Italy (1876); Fatima,

---

30. Rahner, *Visions and Prophecies*, p 84

Portugal (1917) to three children, Lucia, Francisco and Jacinta. Other appearances include Beauraing, Belgium (1932) and Banneux, Belgium (1933) to Mariette Beco.[31] The most popular are the well known sites of Lourdes, Guadalupe, Fatima and Medjugorje, although the latter has not received official approval.[32]

The apparitions at Knock (1879-80) in the West of Ireland are not mentioned in the list above. They were, nonetheless, rooted in the history, culture and social circumstance of their time. Knock, according to James Donnelly, must be situated in the context of the lively local national awareness of the earlier apparitions at Lourdes. Furthermore, he points out that the Knock appearances were, 'against a sombre background of severe agricultural crisis ... in the early months of the [Irish] Land War [1879-1887]'.[33] Knock was but one example of European social and political discontent. David Blackbourn adds: 'There is no doubt that modern apparitions were commonly triggered by larger events: periods of wartime or post-war stress, political conflict and socio-economic crisis.'[34] Evidently, Mary was much more likely to bestow her miracles and appearances on people who lived in politically troubled times and environments but this did not lessen the legitimacy of the beliefs or the devotion of her followers, regardless of their socio-economic background.

Far from the troubles of yesteryear, we also have contemporary highly influential scholars such as René Laurentin who is now generally credulous of them. Having initially sided with the skeptics, he finally spent many years of his life working towards authentication of those apparitions which he thought to be among the most credible. Laurentin emphasises that although ecclesiastical advisers favour prudence and study, Mary's messages are delivered with urgency

31. Jaroslav Pelikan, *Mary Through the Centuries*, New Haven: Yale University Press, 1996

32. See René Laurentin, *The Apparitions of the Blessed Virgin Mary Today*, Dublin: Veritas, 1990

33. James Donnelly, 'The Marian Shrine of Knock: The First Decade', *Eire-Ireland*, Vol XXVIII, No 2 (1993), pp 55, 61.

34. David Blackbourn, *Marpingen, Apparitions of the Virgin Mary in Bismarckian Germany*, Oxford: Clarendon Press, 1993, p 7

justifying devotion to her through the apparitions as acceptable practice. Furthermore, although he respects the need for prudence with regard to scientifically unexplained phenomena, he searches for conventional ways of reclaiming the apparitions so that they are in line with the message of the gospel and church teaching.[35] It is of the utmost importance for Laurentin that the Marian visionaries not only remind the faithful of the very important gospel messages they relay but also that they are heard again in a new way. The apparitions are not an 'add on' to the gospel, they do not supplement it in any way, rather they are significant because they mean to 'remove the scales from our eyes, to reopen our ears, to actualise the gospel, to insert it into our times and show, once more, its power to underline its own life-giving values'.[36]

Mexican theologian Virgil Elizondo also justifies his version of the apparition stories when he exhorts theologians to reinterpret rather than to reject Mary's popular religious symbols. He says that in past decades the tendency of rational theology was to view symbols as fantasies by underlining their ambiguity and then by speaking of them only in negative terms. His concern is that this view, 'leads to an opposition between the religion of the people, which is not looked upon as true faith, and faith in Christ, which appears as the religion of the intellectual elite'.[37] Elizondo has reservations about this dichotomy. If popular devotion and its symbols, including the apparitions, appear uncertain to the theologian that is one thing, but he says that it is through these media that people often relate to the God of Jesus. It is important, pastorally as well as theologically, to try to find the relationship between the meaning of popular symbols and how they function in relation to the gospel.[38] O'Carroll is of the same opinion – to ignore such phenomena, he says, 'is not uniformly edifying; rather it is the policy of the ostrich'.[39]

35. Laurentin, *The Apparitions*, p 15
36. Laurentin, *The Apparitions*, p 19
37. Virgil Elizondo, 'Our Lady of Guadalupe as a Cultural Symbol: The Power of the Powerless', *Concilium*, Vol 2 (1977), p 25
38. Elizondo, 'Our Lady of Guadalupe', p 25
39. Michael O'Carroll, 'Mary Mother of God' in J. Komonchak, M. Collins, D. Lane (eds), *The New Dictionary of Theology*, Dublin: Gill and Macmillan, p 643

What conclusions, then, are to be drawn from the apparitions
and the popular devotion emanating from them? Furthermore,
where do they fit into the equation of Catholic doctrine? Firstly,
the faithful are not bound by church authority either to believe
or disbelieve in the apparitions. Secondly, out of the church's
investigation of more than a thousand of the apparitions, it has
officially recognised only a small proportion of them. Thirdly,
the church authorities prefer to err on the side of caution.
Fourthly, nothing can be added to the revelation of Christ until
the end of time, so whether Mary appears or not is not really the
issue from the church's authoritative position.

How then are the apparitions to be interpreted in the light of
the christatypical approach? Human beings have and will
always appreciate some form of tangibility within the context of
their spiritual lives and the mystery of the unseen God. The
Catholic Church provides that tangibility through its seven
sacraments. Michael Drumm and Tom Gunning liken the
sacraments to 'a door opening onto the very life of God'.[40] They
have intuited that unless the sacraments impact personally and
socially in the lives of those who participate in them, they are
meaningless. They warn: 'The problem is that many people
perceive the sacraments as a closed door rather than the invited
threshold they are intended to be.'[41] Although Drumm and
Gunning endeavour, with considerable success, to revitalise the
meaning of the sacraments and sacramental life for the church
as a whole, clearly that has not been sufficient to ease the
yearning of its faithful members as they aspire to catch a
glimpse of the Beatific Vision. Mary's appearances in human
form point to the tangibility of Christ in human form. Yet he is
taking a long time to revisit and the wait is endless in this cruel
and crumbling world. He will not appear again until the end of
time, but no matter, for Mary as Christatype is the visible,
tangible presence promising her Son's long awaited return.

So far it has been shown how the image of Mary as
Christatype developed through the ages, but now it is timely to
identify two particularly important privileges that reveal the

40. Michael Drumm and Tom Gunning, *A Sacramental People* Vol 1, Dublin:
The Columba Press, 1999, p 11
41. Drumm and Gunning, *A Sacramental People* Vol 1, p 11

christatypical approach most effectively. These are the titles of Co-Redeemer and Mediatrix. Tissa Balasuriya identifies the relationship between the privileges when he says that these, 'two functions of Mary are somewhat distinct from, but closely related to, each other. They both depend on the doctrine of redemption by Jesus Christ.'[42]

Mary as Co-Redeemer
The teaching relating to Mary as Co-Redeemer is complex and difficult. The title lends itself to imaging Mary as Christatype because it categorically situates Mary at the side of Christ in the great mystery of redemption. From around the seventeenth-century, especially in France and Spain, Mary came to be seen either as associate of the Redeemer or Co-Redeemer. The title waxed and waned from that period until the pontificate of Pius XII where it blossomed along with many other titles.[43] Semmelroth's concerns in this respect are evident when he warned theologians around the time of the Second Vatican Council to be, 'careful to steer a middle course between errors of excess and defect'.[44] The difficulty with the Co-Redeemer title is an obvious one since it threatens to confuse Christ's role with Mary's, for she would have to merit with Christ in order to bring about salvation for humankind.

Prior to the Second Vatican Council, there was for centuries an enormous reluctance to take Mary from the side of Christ as his Co-Redeemer, placing a high value on her in relation to the work of redemption. To this end, theologians such as Karl Rahner and Cyril Vollert deliberate with the title. Rahner, for example, substantiates Mary's co-redeemership by imaging her as the perfect human being. Through her unquestionable faith, she stands alone as the, 'ideal representation of exhaustive redemption because of her unique place in saving history'.[45]

42. Tissa Balasuriya, *Mary and Human Liberation*, London: Mowbray, 1997, p 159
43. O' Carroll, 'Mary, Mother of God', p 641
44. Otto Semmelroth, *Mary the Archetype of the Church*, Dublin: Gill and Son, 1964, p 62
45. Karl Rahner, 'The Interpretation of the Dogma of the Assumption', *Theological Investigations* Vol 1, Darton, Longman and Todd, 1965, p 225

Vollert's contribution to the mystery is also worthy of quote where he asks:

> What, then, remains for Mary? Has her presence on Calvary any redemptive meaning? The incarnate Word fully represents humanity; but by God's will, Mary represents aspects of humanity which Christ did not assume. She represents the mere creature, whereas Christ is a divine person; she represents the redeemed, for Christ is not redeemed.[46]

As he focuses on the ambiguity of the role, Vollert locates Mary firmly within the human scheme of things. In this respect, he decides that Mary has, indeed, a role to play but it must not in any way usurp that of Christ. To avoid this predicament, he justifies Mary's position on what is *left over* after Christ has done his redemptive work. However, now we have the anomaly of a perfect creature that appears to be capable of assuming certain aspects of humanity which Christ as Saviour did not himself assume. This is despite the fact that Mary is subordinate to him. It is difficult to see in this reckoning what aspects of humanity could Mary assume that Christ could not?

Another way around the theological dilemma was to advert to the distinction between objective and subjective redemption.[47] However, as Semmelroth has it, a major problem arises for it is difficult to know if Mary co-operated with Christ as *redemptio objectiva* (through Christ's salvific action) or only as *redemptio subjectiva* (through the individual's own free response to salvation). If Mary is to be understood in the light of the former, then she is directly involved with him in the salvific process. This means, of course, that Christ can put salvation into effect only through his mother's co-operation – a concept which Semmelroth finds difficult to sustain since she cannot be a co-worker in her own salvation. There is after all only one means of redemption and that is through the Redeemer. Mary, as with the

---

46. Cyril Vollert, *A Theology of Mary*, Herder and Herder: New York, 1965, p 152

47. See Michael O'Grady, 'Mary's Role in Redemption' in K. McNamara (ed), *Mother of the Redeemer*, Dublin: Gill and Son, 1959, pp 135-158 and Brian Kelly, 'Our Lady and Objective Redemption', *Irish Theological Quarterly*, Vol. XXXIII, No 3 (1966), pp 242-353

rest of humankind, must receive grace and redemption through him alone.[48]

If, on the other hand, Mary co-operated with Christ through *redemptio subjectiva* this is more acceptable provided, however, her co-operation is based on her being imaged as archetype of the church. According to Semmelroth, it would not have been befitting for Mary to have co-operated with redemption in any other way than does the church itself. Here it is clear that Mary's subjective co-redemption is not to be taken in isolation from her role as a member of the church, albeit that she remains a super-eminent one. Her subjective co-redemption must subordinate her to Christ.[49] To this effect, Semmelroth uses an official statement from Pius XII's *Mystici corporis*[50] clarifying his theology of the co-redeemership of all humankind while at the same time including Mary. He clarifies: 'Through the church every man performs a work of collaboration with Christ in dispensing the graces of Redemption, thus acting as "co-redeemer".'[51]

The Second Vatican Council, on its own behalf, refers back to the fathers of the church, stating that they rightly see, 'Mary not merely as passively engaged by God, but as freely *co-operating* (emphasis added) in the work of man's salvation through faith and obedience ... where she devoted herself totally, as a handmaid of the Lord, to the person and work of her Son, under and with him, serving the mystery of redemption, by the grace of Almighty God'.[52] In this way, the Council resolved the matter somewhat by omitting the title 'Co-Redeemer', thereby ensuring that Mary's role in redemption was one that serves 'under and with him'.[53]

Those involved in ecumenical movements, however, still share some concerns about the part played by Mary, even with respect to the use of the word 'co-operation'. Nowhere is this

---

48. Semmelroth, *Mary the Archetype of the Church*, pp 72-74
49. Semmelroth, *Mary the Archetype of the Church*, p 81
50. Pius XII, *Mystici corporis*, New York: The America Press, 1943
51. Cited in Semmelroth, *Mary the Archetype of the Church*, p 82
52. Vatican Council II, *The Counciliar and Post Counciliar Documents, Lumen gentium* in A. Flannery (ed), Dublin: Dominican Publications, 1975, par 56
53. Vatican Council II, *Lumen Gentium*, par 56

clearer than in the joint efforts of the ecumenical Dombes group when they say:

> Since the term 'co-operation' is there and is alive in the mentalities of both sides [i.e. Catholics and Protestants], we cannot act as if it did not exist. Our effort will therefore be to both purify and 'convert' it, to 'reconstruct' it, as it were. Some day, perhaps, a different term will emerge from our dialogue, one that is more satisfactory to all concerned, because it will be free of all equivocations.[54]

The title Co-Redeemer might well have been dropped from post-Vatican II official documentation but the debate continues. The innocuous use of the term 'co-operating' does little to allay the fears of those who do not wish to see Mary usurping Christ's salvific role. Nonetheless, from a christatypical perspective, there is no relationship more indissolubly linked than that of Mary and her Redeemer-son. Being the nearest to Christ, Mary through her grace and vocation as Co-Redeemer, transports the faithful deeper in understanding of the mystery of redemption. Within the context of that mystery as yet, Mary is Christatype.

Mary as Mediatrix
Although there is no clear biblical basis for it, Mary as Mediatrix emerges around the fourth-century, originating in the Eastern Church. Again, like that of co-redeemer, she stands close to Christ as the Christatype, reflecting his mediatory role. One of the earliest accounts of Mary's mediation is found in a hymn by the poet-theologian Ephraim of Syria (AD306-373) in his sweet refrain: 'I call upon you Mediatrix of the World; I invoke your prompt attention to my necessities'.[55] Later at the Council of Ephesus (AD431) the dominant Cyril of Alexandria comes to the fore in reference to Mary's ability to intercede:

> Through thee, the trinity is glorified; through thee, the Cross is venerated in the whole world ... through thee, angels and

---

54. Alain Blancy *et al*, *Mary in the Plan of God and in the Communion of Saints*, New York: Paulist Press, 2002, p 89
55. Cited in Joseph Grassi, *Mary, Mother & Disciple*, Wilmington: Michael Glazier Inc, 1988, pp 125-126

archangels rejoice, through thee, demons are chased ... through thee, the fallen creature is raised to heaven ... through thee, the churches are founded in the whole world, through thee the people are led to conversion.[56]

Attention to Paul's first Letter to Timothy referring to Christ as Mediator between God and people no doubt influenced Cyril *a propos* Mary's mediatory powers (1 Tim 2:5-7). By the twelfth-century, Mary's strengthening position as Mediatrix is becoming ever more palpable. The Benedictine abbot in the diocese of Chartres, Arnold of Bonneval (AD1144-56) believed that the glory of the Mother of God and her Son was indivisible, bestowing their mercy on the faithful between them. Where Christ shows his wounds to God, Mary displays her breasts. It does not stop there, for Mary also shares in the suffering on the cross in her work of the redemption. Bonneval unites her to Christ in a most incredible way, for he claims that, 'there was one single will of Christ and Mary, both together one holocaust to God ... this unity allows no division, nor is it divided into parts, and even though one is made out of two, this cannot henceforth be divided.'[57]

Such was the power of Mary as Mediatrix in the Catholic tradition that the Dombes ecumenical group is concerned to say of the title, 'It has become freighted with considerable mis-understanding.'[58] Nowhere is this clearer than in the words of Belgian theologian Joseph Bittremieux: 'Christ is the main mediator, Mary is a secondary Mediator; thus, Mary's mediatorship must be stressed as parallel to Christ's but none the less subordinate to his.'[59] Although it is not Bittremieux's intention to place Mary on a par with Christ as Mediator, nonetheless he writes of her subordinate yet parallel mediatory position at one and the same time. If we accept the caution of the Dombes ecumenical group that the Mediatrix title is liable to cause confusion, and take into account the voice of a theologian such as Bittremieux, it is not difficult to see how uncertainty might arise.

---

56. Cited in O'Carroll, *Theotokos*, p 113
57. Cited in Graef, *A History of Doctrine and Devotion* Vol 1, p 243
58. Blancy *et. al.*, *Mary*, p 88
59. Cited in Semmelroth, *Mary the Archetype of the Church*, p 81

The title nonetheless remains in church teaching. Unlike that of Co-Redeemer, it is found in Chapter eight of *Lumen Gentium* where the council fathers write: 'The Blessed Virgin is invoked in the church under the titles Advocate, Helper, Benefactress, and Mediatrix.'[60] Insertion of the Mediatrix title into the Council documents did not come without promotion of it. According to O'Carroll, at the pre-conciliar worldwide episcopal consultation, out of 570 future council fathers, 382 wanted a pronouncement on Mary's mediation. The lobby for any other item on the agenda at this time consisted of smaller alignments. If the pro-Mediatrix group thought that the Mediatrix title was about to move smoothly into its place in the council documents, they were mistaken. Instead it only made its way there after contentious debate, confrontation and disappointment.[61]

Certain popes in the past also have shown considerable awareness of the designation and what it meant for their flocks. This Christatype title is evident, for instance, in Pius IX (1846-1878) when he writes:

> ... the safest refuge for all who are in peril, the most trusty aid, and with her only begotten Son, the most powerful Mediatrix and reconciler of the world ... and she with the entreaties of a mother most powerfully pleads our cause – she obtains, too, whatever she asks, and she cannot be disappointed.[62]

Following Pius IX, Pope Leo XIII (1878-1903) wrote: 'Nothing is given us but through Mary – according to God's Will. So we cannot come to the Father except by the Son and we cannot come to the Son but through the Mother.'[63] From Leo's pontificate until that of Pius XII (1939-1958), popes wrote more or less along the same lines in reference to Mary as Mediatrix. Pius XII's christatypical approach in relation to her mediatory role is overt when he says: 'It is God's will that we shall receive

---

60. Vatican Council II, *Lumen gentium*, par 62
61. O'Carroll, 'Mary Mother of God', p 642
62. Cited in Bourke, *The Bull Ineffabilis*, pp 75-76
63. Cited in Michael O'Carroll, *Mediatress of all Graces*, Dublin: Golden Eagle Books, 1959, p 159
64. Cited in O'Carroll, *Mediatress of all Graces*, p 159

all graces through the hands of Mary. This is a very sweet doctrine that all theologians with one accord defend today.'[64]

In the Mediatrix title, then, it can be claimed that the roles of Mary and Christ interconnect with one another, setting Mary firmly within an appreciation of her as Christatype. Mary's people, those who love her, need her and await her answers, through their intercessory prayers have placed her in this position and there she will remain. It may thus be said that generations past and present were influenced by some of the writings and doctrines of certain of the early fathers, theologians and popes who leaned towards imaging Mary as Christatype through the Mediatrix title. Distinctions between the mediatorship of Christ and Mary may at times throughout the centuries have been indistinct but, what does it matter to the beseechers so long as prayers are answered and their much needed petitions hold the hope of a positive response? In fact, what does it matter if the prayers are not answered in the way that is requested, for is it not actually the hope that Mary promises as intercessor and Mediatrix that truly counts? The great Irish bard Séamus Heaney famously wrote of hope:

> History says, Don't hope on this side of the grave. But then once in a lifetime the longed-for tidal wave of justice can rise up and hope and history rhyme.[65]

One of the realities of the human condition is that we need an intercessor, someone whom we can relate to as well as to Christ. No matter how loudly it is proclaimed that Mary is subordinate to him, the distinction is never going to be made quite so readily by those who have had and continue to have a deep and trusting relationship with her. This does not imply that they would overtly refute the scriptural foundation of Christ as Mediator, 'For there is one God, and there is one who brings God and mankind together, the man Christ Jesus, who gave himself to redeem all mankind' (1 Tim 2:5-7). However, Mary's title as Mediatrix is firmly set in the context of the christatypical approach. Those who wish to image her in this way recognise her inestimable value as one who stands most closely at the side of Christ – a privilege not available to lesser mortals.

65. Séamus Heaney, *The Cure at Troy*, London: Faber and Faber, 1990, p 7

The Assumption

Unlike the titles of Mary as Co-Redeemer and Mediatrix, her assumption into heaven was proclaimed a dogma. The dogma of the assumption is being categorised as christatypical because it reflects, albeit in a lesser way, both the ascension and the resurrection of Christ. Clearly the woman who had given birth to the Saviour could not have been left to die and putrefy. Mary died but it was not an end – Jesus died but it was not an end. Certainly all Christians believe that death is not the end. In faith they believe they will be raised from the dead, but that will not parallel the assumption of Mary or the resurrection of Christ. In that sense, it could be argued that it sets Mary in the context of christological privilege. Throughout the centuries, belief in the assumption increased universally and in popularity among the faithful, who desired some kind of formal promulgation by church authority. Assuming that O'Carroll's statistics are correct, he explains how:

> Down to the year 1941 the dogmatic definition of Our Lady's Assumption was requested by one hundred and thirteen cardinals, over three hundred archbishops and bishops, some thirty-two thousand priests and brothers, fifty thousand religious women, and by more than eight million of the laity.[66]

Despite the clamouring for official recognition, considerable complexity is attached to this dogma. Hans Küng, for example, is wary of the universal binding of a dogmatic definition that was developed extraneous to biblical factors. Furthermore, he criticises the habit of the popes from Pius IX to Pius XII who promoted Marian devotion by every means possible. Sounding like someone from the heady days of the Protestant Reformation, he claims that since, 'the nineteenth century Marianism and papalism have gone hand in hand and given each other mutual support'.[67] The peak of the Marian age came in 1950 with the proclamation of the dogma of the assumption which he sees as a papal swansong in a last effort to practice absolute power over against, 'all Protestant, Orthodox and even Catholic misgivings'.[68]

---

66. O'Carroll, *Mediatress of All Graces*, p 262
67. Hans Küng, *On Being a Christian*, London: Collins, 1974, p 461
68. Küng, *On Being a Christian*, p 461

Whether or not the church authorities used the teaching of the assumption of Mary for vainglorious purposes is not for discussion here, nor is it possible to agree definitively with the veracity of Küng's claim. Nonetheless, it is legitimate to ask why this doctrine, without scriptural foundation, became so important to the life of the church that it was proclaimed a dogma with binding infallible status.

How did the dogma come about? According to the Spanish theologian Joseph Paredes, there was nothing of any serious doctrinal consequence to be found in the first five centuries after Christ.[69] As the sixth-century dawned, a growing conviction was emerging among the faithful that Mary's body and soul went to heaven. It was from this time onwards that her assumption was celebrated on 15 August. Between the eighth and the eleventh centuries, Mary was held to be deeply physically united with Christ through her bodily assumption. It was only appropriate, therefore, that Mary be glorified with her Son and what better way to justify her assumption into heaven than through scriptural reference. However, despite no account of Mary's assumption being recorded in the New Testament, quotations from scripture issued fairly fluently from about the thirteenth-century onwards.

Credence in Mary's assumption continued until 1950 when it was proclaimed a dogma by Pius XII. In the years proximate to the proclamation, theological discussion on the matter, according to Marie Farrell, was contentious, particularly as it was not supported either by scripture or patristic literature (c. AD100-451).[70] The complication emanates from three interpretative phases applying to it. The first phase (1854-1950) witnessed attempts to interpret the assumption only in terms of the Immaculate Conception, the latter which was defined as a dogma in 1854. Given that death is punishment for sin and Mary

---

69. See Joseph Paredes, *Mary and the Kingdom of God*, Middlegreen: St Paul Publications, 1990, pp 232-241. Mary's assumption also occurs in the apocryphal gospels between the fourth and the sixth centuries. These stories give an account of her death and assumption.

70. Marie Farrell, 'The Assumption of Mary – Prophetic Symbol for a Pilgrim People', *The Australasian Catholic Record*, Vol LXIX, No 3 (1992), p 321

was without sin, it was inappropriate for her to suffer the consequence of sin. The concentration, therefore, was placed on a doctrine which could be associated with her passing from its sinless condition.[71] This phase came to a close in 1950 with the decree of Pius XII and the following decree:

> We proclaim, declare and define it to be a dogma revealed by God that the Immaculate Mother of God, Mary ever Virgin, when the course of her earthly life was finished, was taken up body and soul into the glory of heaven.[72]

The second phase (1950-1964) did not concentrate singularly on Mary and her privileges. Instead, it focused on an interpretation of her life in relation to the whole of humanity as one who would experience the fruits of Christ's redemption. This gave the assumption an eschatological thrust which was the final in a series of transitions marking Mary's life. Within that context, the annunciation represented a move from pre-Christian to Christian times. Calvary represented a shift from a state of pre-church to complete ecclesial reality and the assumption represented the final union of the entire church within the risen Christ. Farrell asserts that both these eschatological and soteriological views were supplemented by, 'Otto Semmelroth's particular use of ecclesiology in order to show how the assumption may be considered by the *typos* of bodily redemption for the whole church'.[73]

The cumulative effect of using such a method, that is, one which universalised the assumption, was intended to highlight meaning about the church – a method adopted by the fathers of the Second Vatican Council.[74] The following headings in chapter eight of *Lumen gentium* make the point: 'The Function of the Blessed Virgin in the Plan of Salvation';[75] 'The Blessed Virgin and the Church';[76] 'the Cult of the Blessed Virgin in the Church'[77]

---

71. Farrell, 'The Assumption of Mary', p 325
72. Pius XII, *Munificentissimus Deus*, Dublin: Irish Messenger Office, 1950, par 44
73. Farrell, 'The Assumption of Mary', p 325
74. Semmelroth, *Mary the Archetype of the Church*, pp 243-175
75. Vatican Council II, *Lumen gentium*, par 55
76. Vatican Council II, *Lumen gentium*, par 60
77. Vatican Council II, *Lumen gentium*, par 66

and 'Mary, Sign of Hope and Comfort for the Pilgrim People of God'.[78] The third phase (1964-1970s) retained the universalising soteriological and eschatological compounds of the second phase. This post-Vatican II period coincided with the development of an ecclesiology which had begun to recognise that the church was a far greater reality than a mere institution.[79]

Nonetheless, it is being argued here that the dogma of the assumption more readily portrays a stronger christological than an ecclesiological orientation. As Farrell puts it, 'The dogma of the assumption refers, first and foremost, to the saving mystery of God in Christ.'[80] The history of the exceptionally close relationship between Christ and Mary through her assumption continues today, revealing that it fits in well with Mary as christatype. Rahner, it could be said, helps that point to come across when he suggests that the dogma in fact belongs to the article of faith that Christ was, 'born of the Virgin Mary'.[81] This article directs us to a *saving event* for the whole world – one which took place in and through the flesh of Mary, so much so that our salvation depends upon Christ's having been born of her. Or in Rahner's words: 'She lets the Son of God into the world ... But he graced her in just such a way that in her (flesh and faith together) the salvation of the world has definitively begun ...'[82]

As if in a continuous chain of mystical events, Mary's assumption is also associated with Christ's ascension. This connection is a familiar theme in the tradition. To explain the distinction between the two, Macquarrie draws attention to the linguistic characteristics of the word 'assumption'. He explains that:

As a 'taking up', an assumption ... is an act of God, in the performance of which the person assumed remains passive. On the other hand, an ascension ... means 'going up' and is a word which gives an active role to the person who goes up.[83]

78. Vatican Council II, *Lumen gentium*, par 68
79. Farrell, 'The Assumption of Mary', pp 325-326
80. Farrell, 'The Assumption of Mary', pp 325-326
81. Rahner, K., 'The Interpretation of the Dogma of the Assumption', *Theological Investigations* Vol 1, London: DLT, 1965, p 217.
82. Rahner, 'Interpretation', Vol.1, *TI*, p 217
83. John Macquarrie, *Mary for All Christians*, London: Collins, 1991, p 81

Macquarrie, a one time a member of the Church of Scotland and then a member of the Anglican Communion, wishes to make clear that the only person who ascended to God of his own accord was Christ. Although he justifies his belief in the assumption of Mary on the grounds that her body could not be allowed just to corrupt in the earth, his concern is to show that the assumption is not a glorification of Mary. To think of it in these terms would be to infringe that place which belongs to Christ alone.[84] Compare this to Boff, from the Catholic Christian tradition, describing Mary's risen body as being, 'enthroned in celestial glory'.[85] For him, the assumption means that Mary reigns beside her Son where they abide in love and union beyond our human imagining.[86] Official church teaching runs along the same lines. Vatican Council II teaches that Mary, 'was taken up body and soul into heavenly glory, when her earthly life was over, and exalted by the Lord as Queen over all things that she might be the more fully conformed to her Son'.[87] This glorification of Mary, then, which arises out of a belief in the glorious assumption, puts Mary alongside Christ. Mary's assumption strikes a parallel with Christ's resurrection and glorious ascension, and it is through these mysteries that Mary is imaged as Christatype.

Conclusion

What then is to be said of Mary as Christatype? Primarily we argue that it was one way of imaging Mary or an approach which began to emerge at a time when the early fathers were trying to fathom more profoundly Christ's role and function in the mystery of salvation. We do well to remember that, from the beginning of Christianity until the early fourth-century, Mary was never at the heart of theological deliberations. We recall that any statements in reference to her were always principally statements about Christ. Leahy tells us that: 'In theological reflection Mary remained in the background, as it were, until

---

84. Macquarrie, *Mary for All Christians*, pp 83-84
85. Boff, *The Maternal Face of God*, p 171
86. Boff, *The Maternal Face of God*, pp 171-172
87. Vatican Council II, *Lumen gentium*, par 59

Christ's divine identity was fully expressed at the Council of Nicea (AD325) and his relationship to the church as redeemer clarified.'[88] During that early period of debate and fear of heresies, theological argumentation about the nature of Christ was rife and, by extension, certain ambiguities accrued around the role of Mary in the grand scheme of salvation. The theological uncertainty that flourished admitted of her human frailties but, at one and the same time, elevated her to a position very close to Christ. Mary's role eventually became so inter-twined with Christ's that she was imaged as standing at his side facing his people.

As time passed, Mary often came to be seen as one to whom the faithful could relate, particularly during the harshest of times in human history. Her proximity to Christ revealed the face of Christ, but there was no point in turning to him exclusively for assistance and succour if Mother was going to be easier to persuade. Not only was Mary available in the minds of the tumultuous generations of peoples, but she was also willing to appear in tangible form in places where she could be visited and might even appear again. She began to perform miracles – yes so did Jesus of Nazareth, but that was two thousand years ago. Now that he was in heaven and the Second Person of the Blessed Trinity, he would no longer appear on earth to perform miracles or show his face in human form. He will appear again, of course, but only at the end of time. Instead, through God, Mary comes in Christ's place, and who knows where or when she will appear again? She can appear many times and at any time – she does not have to wait until the last days. Not only does she perform miracles and offer much needed hope, but she also has the ability to co-redeem, co-mediate and to act as intercessor between humankind and God. In this way she is imaged as the Christatype.

---

88. Leahy, *The Marian Profile*, p 21

CHAPTER THREE

They Called Her Church

And has Our Lady lost her place? Does her white star burn dim?
Nay, she has lowly veiled her face because of him.[1]

Mary as Ecclesiatype

Put simply, Mary as Ecclesiatype identifies her as 'one of us'
where she is situated firmly among the human race within the
milieu of the church as the People of God. She walks with us,
prays with us, stands beside us and sustains us as we endeavour
to go about our earthly lives. In this sense, members of the faith
community accept Mary as a woman of great compassion and
one to whom they can turn in time of need primarily because of
her shared capacity for human empathy. Emphasis on her
humanity is at the very kernel of comprehending the ecclesiatypical approach. Those who see her in this way recognise her
human frailties and limitations, albeit as the Mother of God
Incarnate. We must, however, compare the average lifespan of
the human being with the lifespan of Mary. Hers has traversed
the centuries where ours is more or less 'three score years and
ten'. In this sense, she is a two-thousand year old human
phenomenon and it is within the context of her eternal presence
that the image of Mary as Ecclesiatype is to be understood. The
subject of her status in this chapter is not about the grandeur of
the theatypical or christatypical ways of imaging Mary as we
have seen in the previous two chapters. Rather we search again
for evidence of the ecclesiatypical approach among the early
fathers, some ancient theologians and documents from the
magisterium of the late twentieth-century. Reference will also
be made to the Marian deliberations of the Anglican Roman
Catholic International Commission.

Specifically, firstly it will be shown that the nucleus of Mary

---

1. Kennedy, 'Good Friday Falls on Lady Day', p 98

as Ecclesiatype originated (like the previous two approaches) with the early fathers. Secondly, emphasis will be placed on the Second Vatican Council's attempt to locate Mary within the wider framework of the economy of salvation as found in chapter eight of *Lumen gentium*. Thirdly, consideration will be taken of the part played by the council in reference to Mary's place in ecumenism, with brief reference to subsequent ecumenical endeavours. Finally, attention will paid to the long shadows cast by Pope Paul VI and Pope John Paul II whose writings, it will be argued, are all variously grounded (although not exclusively) in the image of Mary as Ecclesiatype. Each of these in turn will provide a useful frame of reference for our understanding of the ecclesiatypical approach which will bear greater fruit of its meaning in the final chapter. Essential elements pertaining to imaging Mary as Ecclesiatype, such as her historicity, her faith and her discipleship, will be outlined and developed at that stage. The most important element of all within that context is the emphasis on is her human nature.

The Ecclesiatype Emerging

One of the earliest texts in reference to Mary's humanity is found in Paul's letter to the Galatians where he writes: 'But when the right time finally came, God sent his own Son. He came as the Son of a human mother and lived under the Jewish law' (Gal 4:4). In this verse, Paul's concern above all is to stress the moment when Jesus became a member of the human race. In doing so, he refers indirectly to Mary where, according to Raymond Brown, 'it is a reference to her simply as mother, in her maternal role of bearing Jesus and bringing him into the world'.[2] Paul is so unconcerned with Mary that he does not even name her, permitting the Russian Orthodox theologian Elisabeth Behr-Sigel, commenting on Galatians 4:4, to state that: 'Mary is not a feminine divinity. She is the completely human mother of God ...'[3]

---

2. Raymond Brown *et al*, *Mary in the New Testament*, New York: Paulist Press, 1978, p 43
3. Elizabeth Behr-Sigel, 'Mary and Women' in M. Plekon *et al.* (eds), *Discerning the Sign of the Times: The Vision of Elisabeth Behr-Sigel*, New York: St Vladimir's Seminary Press, 2001, p 108

Taking this further, in his exegesis of Paul's phrase, Lawrence Cunningham makes the point that, 'It would be a gigantic conceptual reach to argue for the legitimacy of other Marian doctrines – her virgin birth or, even more her immaculate conception or her bodily assumption into heaven … based on a … meditation of Galatians 4:4.'[4] It has already been shown that Paul had some serious difficulties with the adherents of syncretistic religion – a faith that is created from the merger of concepts from two or more religions and its goddesses. For this reason, it would appear that he was keen to avoid placing too strong an emphasis particularly on Mary's virginity, fearing that unacceptable parallels would be drawn between her and the goddesses of the day such as Isis (Egypt), Kybele (Rome) and Demeter (Greek). Hence Paul's allusion to Mary comes to the fore as 'woman' or 'human mother' depending on the translation.

Relatively shortly after Paul's time, Ignatius Bishop of Antioch (d. c. AD110) makes reference to Mary's humanity and its significance for the birth of Christ. Ignatius feared the dreaded gnostic heresy and its docetic teaching – docetism is derived from the Greek *dokeo*, to seem. It is the belief that Christ only seemed to be human and did not really have a body. As his best defence, Ignatius thus stressed the true birth of Jesus from the womb of Mary, emphasising the reality of her childbirth by saying that, 'Jesus Christ … was 'out of' Mary, who was truly born'.[5] Approximately one hundred years later, reference to Mary's humanity is found again in Irenaeus (d. c. AD200) where, according to Sally Cunneen, 'he sees Mary as a human being, someone perhaps like his own mother. Neither devotion nor dogma separates her from other women. Irenaeus associates Mary closely with humanity and the church.'[6]

A phenomenon which corresponds to the human condition is that of human suffering and one to which, according to Epiphanius (d. AD403), Mary was very much susceptible. With

---

4. Lawrence Cunningham, 'Born of a Woman (Gal 4:4): A Theological Meditation' in C. E. Braaten and R.W. Jenson (eds), *Mary Mother of God*, Cambridge: Eerdmans Publishing Company, 2004, p 45
5. Cited in Graef, *A History of Doctrine and Devotion*, Vol 1, p 34
6. Sally Cunneen, *In Search of Mary: The Woman and the Symbol*, New York: Ballantine Books, 1996, p 66

respect to her suffering and subsequent death, he suggests that she may have even been martyred and died violently – at least such is his interpretation of the Sword of Simeon prophecy (Lk 2:35).[7] Certainly in one of his contemporaries, Augustine (AD 354-430), we find no doubt of Mary's suffering, again on account of the same prophecy. Augustine has it that the sword which pierced her soul was the grief she experienced when she witnessed her Son's death at Calvary. She was so overwhelmed by his agony that she did not dare even to presume his resurrection. In respect of her human condition, Augustine does not make any distinction between Mary, her suffering and what befalls other members of the church, for she is a part of the church although not yet a member of the whole body. Mary is but a holy member of whom Christ is both the head and the body.[8]

The themes of Mary's human sorrows and suffering continue into the sixth-century as seen in the prayer to Christ of the Syrian poet Jacob of Sarug:

> Many sorrows has your Mother borne for your sake, and all afflictions surrounded her at your crucifixion. How many sorrowing weepings and tears of suffering did not her eyes shed at your funeral … How many terrors did not the Mother of Mercy experience when you were buried and the guards of the sepulchre turned her away, so that she could not approach you.[9]

Aside from suffering, other human characteristics and frailties such as confusion and lack of knowledge on Mary's part about her Son's reason for existence, are evident in some few writings of the early centuries of Christianity. Although he had

---

7. See O'Carroll, *Theotokos*, p 387. O'Carroll says that there are many interpretations of this prophecy which has puzzled theologians for centuries. Some thought that it forecast a breakdown in Mary's faith during the passion. Other interpretations include: the failure of Israel to establish itself unanimously under Mary's protection, doubt or scandal during the passion, the last judgement, the sword of the angels at the gates of paradise, God's Word searching human hearts or simply Mary's maternal sorrow during the passion.

8. Cited in Graef, *A History of Doctrine and Devotion*, Vol 1, pp 96-97

9. Cited in Graef, *A History of Doctrine and Devotion*, Vol 1, p 122

no doubts whatsoever about the unusual and spirit-filled circumstance of Mary's virginity, John Chrysostom (d. c. AD 349-407) uses as many scriptural references as he can to stress Mary's faults and human imperfections.[10] In his exegesis of Matthew 12:46-50 and its parallel Mark 3:31, where Mary and the brothers of Jesus come to visit Jesus, Chrysostom accuses Mary of unbelief. He goes even further with the annunciation story (Lk 1:26), insisting that Mary would have killed herself upon hearing such unbelievable news had the message about her impending childbirth not been authenticated. Although Chrysostom certainly believed in Mary's miraculous child-bearing and her place in the plan of redemption, he nevertheless saw her as an ordinary woman with typically human traits and weaknesses. As such, Mary deserved to be reproved by her Son whenever that was necessary. Chrysostom's intention was simply to help the faithful appreciate how difficult it was for her to lead a blameless life. If this were the circumstance for the Mother of the Son of God, then how much greater the effort would be required for the rest of humankind who could not lay stake to such a lofty claim.[11]

Mary's humanity in the context of her motherhood is to be found also in Ambrose (AD339-397) but here he extends that concept to the church, specifically as the Body of Christ. He is one of the first church fathers to announce this idea explicitly when he says, 'she is betrothed, yet a virgin, because she is a type of the church, which is immaculate yet married'.[12] For Ambrose, Mary's identification with the church comes to her through suffering as a mother at the foot of the cross. In the same way that Mary gives birth to Christ, she also gives birth to Christians. He insists that both Christ and the church were born from her womb and, as she bows broken beneath the cross, she actually *is* the church. This inspiration comes to him when he ponders the breathless words of the crucified Jesus to the Beloved Disciple and to Mary that they should behold one another (Jn 19:25-27). In Ambrose's interpretation, Mary is not

---

10. See J. N. D. Kelly, *Golden Mouth: The Story of John Chrysostom –*
Ascetic, Preacher, Bishop, Ithaca: Cornell University Press, 1995
11. Cited in Graef, *A History of Doctrine and Devotion*, Vol 1, pp 74-85
12. Cited in Graef, *A History of Doctrine and Devotion*, Vol 1, p 85

only the seed of the church but she is also the personification of it; she is the conceiver of both Christ and of the church. Augustine too affirms Mary's intimate relationship with the church, for when she gave birth to Christ she gave birth to the faithful. He tells them, 'Mary gave birth to your Head, the church to you. For she (the church), too is both mother and virgin'.[13] Mary, for Augustine, evolves from being merely an individual woman to becoming a prototype of the church. In his theology of Mary, she is not above the church although she is its most eminent member.[14]

Belief in the relationship between Mary and the church did not wane but continued through the Dark and early Middle Ages (c. AD476-1000). One such example is found in the English priest, monk and scholar the Venerable Bede (AD672-735) where he is concerned to exemplify Mary as a particularly useful role model for monks and nuns. Given her humility and chastity, he portrays an ecclesiatypical approach in his comparison of Mary and the church. Like others before him, he also makes reference to the Sword of Simeon story to express his conviction that Mary suffers through her relationship with the church. In much the same way as she suffers at the cross, the church endures the same through its persecutions. Not only does Bede associate Mary with the church and focuses on her human suffering, but he emphasises her humility, presenting her as an earthly rather than as a heavenly character.[15]

The above writers, some influential and some not, support evidence that Mary was very much to be counted among the church's human membership. They emphasise that, like every other human being, she suffers as the rest of humankind does and is, therefore, capable of empathising in every way with the trials and tribulations of those who follow Christ. Those writers, then, describe Mary's special association with the church while not excluding her relationship with God through Christ. Furthermore, they reveal that Mary's association with the church is an intimate one, permitting easy access to her by all of its other members. In that light, we now turn to a more

13. Cited in Graef, *A History of Doctrine and Devotion*, Vol 1, p 98
14. Cited in Graef, *A History of Doctrine and Devotion*, Vol 1, p 98
15. Cited in Graef, *A History of Doctrine and Devotion*, Vol 1, pp 162-163

contemporary understanding of Mary as Ecclesiatype and that same association with the church. The next section relates to the later part of the twentieth-century and the second half of chapter eight of the Second Vatican Council's Dogmatic Constitution on the Church, *Lumen gentium*.[16]

Vatican Council II: The Ecclesiatype Developing
It is well known that the council was divided in its opinion about Mary's role in the church. The divergence of views centred on whether or not to include a chapter on Mary in the *Dogmatic Constitution on the Church* or to prepare a separate schema of her own.[17] The controversial debate was reflected in language taken from the turn of the twentieth-century to describe two poles of thought known as the 'maximalist' and the 'minimalist' positions. The maximalists tended to place more emphasis on traditional interpretations of scripture, apparitions and seeking out new feasts and devotions to Mary. The minimalists, on the other hand, were opposed to an over-emphasis on her elevated role in the mystery of redemption and excessive devotion, which was abroad among the faithful and many of the church leaders of the day. These catch phrases ably portrayed the divergent points of view on mariology among the council fathers at the time. Anne Carr expresses the discord by explaining that the maximalists were understood to favour a separate council document for Mary, giving her the elevated position she deserved, whereas the minimalists could be reproved for sacrificing her to ecumenical sensitivities in the interests of church unity.[18]

The two terms also indicated that emphasis on Mary's role in the church would centre more strongly *either* on her christological *or* on her ecclesiological status. Those in favour of christological status tended to be referred to as the 'maximalists' and those in favour of an ecclesiological position were more

16. Vatican Council II, *Lumen gentium*, pars 60-69
17. Anne Carr, 'Mary in the Mystery of the Church Vatican Council 11' in C.F. Jegen (ed), *Mary According to Women*, Kansas City: Sheed and Ward, 1985, p 10
18. Anne Carr, *Transforming Grace*, San Francisco: Harper and Row, 1988, pp 10-11

likely to be labelled as 'minimalists'. It may seem strange now that bishops would engage in a wrestle of wills over the Blessed Virgin Mary, of all things, but there was a very real concern that these diverging viewpoints would split the council into two opposing groups. Michael Novak's well coined phrase gives an indication of how volatile the situation was in the Vatican when he says that the week before the vote on Mary was taken was the, 'blackest week of the Council ... the winds of forward motion had dropped ... and storms were forming in the dark'.[19]

Elizabeth Johnson accesses the kernel of that debate when she explains that:

> The struggle between the two schools of thought can be seen by the 'nevertheless' structure of many paragraphs. For example, the document states that Mary's unique role in salvation as mother of the incarnate Redeemer gives her a special relationship to the triune God (christotypical).'At the same time, however, because she belongs to the offspring of Adam, she is one with all human beings in their need for salvation' (ecclesiotypical, §53). United with her Son in the work of salvation from his birth to her presence at his side in heaven (christotypical), she nevertheless did not understand his reply when she found him in the temple but pondered it in her heart (ecclesiotypical, §57).[20]

The christotypical distinction, therefore, was advocated by those who favoured a Christ-centred mariology, while the ecclesiotypical difference was the choice of those who leaned towards an ecclesiological mariology. Eventually a vote was taken where 1,074 delegates were in favour of a separate *schema* for Mary and 1,114 were supportive of her being included in the dogmatic Constitution on the Church, *Lumen gentium*. The narrow margin of 40 votes worried the minimalists for fear that the 'maximalists' would continue to work to elevate Mary as was their wont. If this were to happen, not only would the council's decision be reversed but the move towards ecumenism would be threatened – a burning issue at the time. On the other

19. Michael Novak, *The Open Church*, London: DLT, 1964, p 176
20. Elizabeth Johnson, *Truly Our Sister*, New York: Continuum, 2003, p 129

hand, concerns were raised by the 'maximalists' that Mary's status would be reduced in a way that was unacceptable to the faithful. For these reasons, according to Cunningham, the 'council's dogmatic constitution on the church admonished theologians, when discussing the Blessed Virgin Mary, to avoid, "all false exaggerations" ... and equally ..."a too narrow mentality" ... when considering the special dignity of the Mother of God'.[21] The council's decision not to warrant Mary with a *schema* of her own has been heavily debated and it has often been credited (or discredited depending on the viewpoint) with a reduction in devotion to Mary. Anne Loades, for example, would say that there are those who would claim that the council was responsible for, 'cutting Mary down to size'.[22]

However, those who agreed with the council's renewal of Marian doctrine did not accept that this was a 'diminishment' of Mary. Rather it was simply a way of expressing a move away from the isolationist mariology prior to the council. One commentator, John Berry, puts it this way:

> This relationship between Marian dogma and other aspects of the faith was a truth which the Second Vatican Council was at pains to stress in its treatment of mariology. It has often been remarked how deeply significant it was that the teaching on Mary was located firmly within the Dogmatic Constitution *Lumen gentium*, its central document on the church. Thus mariology and ecclesiology are seen to be inseparable in the Catholic understanding, and this truth was made abundantly clear in the chapter on 'the role of the Blessed Virgin Mary in the economy of salvation'.[23]

The excerpt shows that significant attempts were made by the council to focus on two theological axes – Mary's relationship with her Son and also her position within the church. In this way, the council attempted to devise ways to

---

21. Cunningham, 'Born of a Woman (Gal 4:4): A Theological Meditation', p 36

22. Anne Loades, 'The Virgin Mary and the Feminist Quest' in J. Soskice (ed), *After Eve*, London: Collins, 1990, p 162

23. John Berry, '*Redemptoris mater* and the Challenge of the Marian Year', *Priests and People*, Vol 1, No 7 (1987), p 270

give, 'unto Christ the things that are Christ's and give unto Mary the things that are Mary's' without confusing the theological elements pertaining to each. In doing so, the council fathers emphasised not only Mary's ecclesiological role but also her christological one.

Vatican Council II: Christ and Mary

Although the council was determined that the roles of Christ and Mary were not to be confused, they had to take into account the integral nature of that relationship. Even more importantly, however, it was incumbent on the council that Christ be portrayed ever and always as the primary focus of the church's teaching. To this end, statements about Christ abounded with the intention of establishing among the faithful an understanding of the universality of the Reign of God, the role of the historical Jesus in that context and his unique involvement with humankind through the dual nature not only of his humanity but also his divinity. The importance of this teaching is evident from the council's statement:

> For, by his incarnation, he, the son of God, has in a certain way united himself with each man. He worked with human hands, he thought with a human mind. He acted with a human will, and with a human heart he loved. Born of the Virgin Mary, he has truly been made one of us, like to us in all things except sin.[24]

Here the council was reinforcing not only the divinity of Jesus but also it was echoing particularly what the Council of Chalcedon (AD451) had taught about his humanity, advising the faithful that Jesus is not to be separated from the historical, religious or social situation of his time.[25] This teaching on Christ's humanity is of singular importance in understanding the human and historical Mary as Ecclesiatype, and in that context we first take account of the meaning of Christ's humanity with reference to the incarnation. The complex mystery of the doctrine of the incarnation is explained by Lane in uncomplic-

24. Vatican Council II, *Gaudium et spes,* par 22
25. Lane, *The Reality of Jesus,* pp 104-108

ated terms where he clarifies that, 'This is usually expressed in the story of God coming down from heaven and entering fully into the human condition in the life and death of Jesus.'[26]

Lane deliberates on the debate between the Jesus of history and the Christ of faith beginning with an investigation of a low ascending christology. He elucidates: 'In practical terms this means beginning with the man Jesus through a process of historical enquiry that will lead to an understanding of the confession of Jesus as Christ and Lord and a discovery of its subsequent universal implications.'[27] This is often referred to as a christology 'from below' or an 'ascending christology', where one's starting point is based on reports of the historical Jesus before consideration of any dogmatic propositions take place. These reports, Lane continues, in part, are gleaned from the gospels. Although they do not give us a chronological account of the life of Jesus they, 'present us primarily with a faith-picture of the early church's experience and understanding of Jesus who is the Christ and the risen Lord'.[28]

Not only does the significance of a low ascending christology permit a return to the historical Jesus, we contend here, but it also enables the faithful to perceive more clearly the advantages of a low ascending mariology. The Mary of history is the travelling companion to those who must live out their lives as she did on this earth in faith, hope and love. A considerable contribution is made by Rahner to our understanding of the meaning of a low ascending mariology when he emphasises that the salvation of humankind primarily occurred in the death-resurrection of Jesus[29] and not as a consequence of Mary's response to the Angel Gabriel (Luke 1:38) through her *fiat* or free will as earlier writings of his advised.[30] Rather, it is very much the free will of the historical Jesus, through suffering and death on the cross, which is the rightful focus for salvation. Once Jesus

26. Dermot Lane, *Christ at the Centre*, Dublin: Veritas, 1990, p 130
27. Lane, *The Reality of Jesus*, p 18
28. Lane, *The Reality of Jesus*, p 19
29. Karl Rahner, 'Christology Today', *Theological Investigations* Vol 21, London: DLT, 1988, p 223
30. Karl Rahner, 'The Immaculate Conception', Theological Investigations Vol 1, London: DLT, 1965, p 206

is at the centre of the salvific process, Christians are then in a position to encounter the human Mary through an ascending Marian theology which permits her 'yes' at the annunciation. This means that her *fiat* is only to be supported within the context of her humanity as she herself tries to comprehend the great mystery of salvation. Mary's 'yes' is now better understood in the light of all those who are in awe of the great mystery of the conception, life, death and resurrection of Christ.

It must be stated categorically, however, that an exact parallel between a low ascending mariology and a low ascending christology cannot be sustained. If this were the case, then there would be something incongruous and over simplistic about the parallel. To begin with, a low ascending christology leads from the humanity of Jesus to the mystery of Christ as God. Or, as Lane reminds us, an ascending christology, 'through the doctrine of the incarnation stands at the centre of the Christian faith and is the bedrock for our understanding of the major truths of Christianity: the Trinity, the church, the sacraments, grace, and eschatology'.[31] The same cannot be said of an ascending mariology, for Mary – even as Mother of God incarnate – must remain within the limits of her historicity. A low ascending mariology does not eliminate her from the vital role she has played in the life of the church, or indeed deny that she is rooted in the incarnation which is the primary purpose of her existence. Account must be taken of the fact that Christ was born of her. Cahal Daly accesses the very great significance of Mary's life when he says: 'Without a woman, the truth of the incarnation could not be realised and our redemption could not have been effected. The church was led to make statements of faith about Mary, not in order to add something to her faith in Christ, but simply in order to maintain her faith in Christ.'[32]

Vatican Council II: Mary and Ecumenical Endeavours
Integral to understanding Mary as Ecclesiatype is the council's decree on ecumenism which triggered a sea-change in the church's

---

31. Lane, *Christ at the Centre*, p 130
32. Cahal Daly, 'Mary and the Church' in J. Hyland (ed), *Mary in the Church*, Dublin: Veritas, 1989, p 139

approach to Marian theology. The council's deliberations on ecumenism are significant because they admitted of the divisions between the various Christian traditions, evident from its introductory ecumenical statement:

> The restoration of unity among all Christians is one of the principal concerns of the Second Vatican Council ... many Christian communions present themselves to men as the true followers of the Lord but they differ in mind and go their different ways, as if Christ himself were divided. Certainly, such division openly contradicts the will of Christ, scandalises the world, and damages the most holy cause, the preaching of the gospel to every creature.[33]

At all costs the council was determined to move forward with its decree on ecumenism, and nowhere was this more obvious than in its re-evaluation of the church's teaching on Mary. It is well known that Marian theology has made it difficult for those of the Catholic and Protestant faith traditions to come together. The primary problem for the latter is the lack of clear basis in scripture of the dogmas of the Immaculate Conception (1854) and the Assumption (1950) and the dissatisfaction with papal authority in reference to the definitions which promulgated them. The council had to re-think its Marian theology, particularly if the decree on ecumenism were to work. Yet, changing attitudes among many within the church was to prove elusive particularly because of the significance of the dogmas to Catholic Christianity and the important contribution they had made to Mary's elevation in the years subsequent to their promulgation. So the council, without reneging on these dogmas, wanted to set mariology on a path that would sustain an ecumenical balance about Mary in its teachings. At least, this was the opinion of those who did not want Marian triumphalism to excel either in theological discourse or in devotion to her among the faithful.

Would it be true to say that although there can be no doubt that the Second Vatican Council was the watershed for new

---

33. Vatican Council II, *The Counciliar and Post-Counciliar Documents, Unitatis redintegratio,* par 1

ecumenical thinking, it was Mary who paid the price for its deliberations?[34] Certainly, as we have seen, efforts were made to steer clear of any excessive devotion which might be likely to overturn its decision in the interests of ecumenism. Paul VI, for example, clearly was careful. An excerpt from the first official document written on Mary by that pope since the council was closed states:

> ... the ecumenical aspect of Marian devotion is shown in the Catholic Church's desire that, without in any way detracting from the unique character of this devotion, every care should be taken to avoid any exaggeration which could mislead other Christian brethren about the true doctrine of the Catholic Church.[35]

In addition, huge ecumenical initiatives were set in train by the Second Vatican Council and the Secretariat for Promoting Christian Unity. This was made easier by a thaw in ecumenical dialogue which had set in well before the council began and was progressing well particularly between Catholicism and Anglicanism. The easing up of the relationships between the two is described thus by Alberic Stacpoole:

> The clear milestones are these: first, the Resolutions of the ten-yearly Lambeth Conferences, of which the most influential was the 1920 Appeal for Christian unity; and secondly, the visits of the Archbishops of Canterbury to the Popes in the Vatican – reconnoitred in 1944 by William Temple ... [the] visit by Geoffrey Fisher to John XXIII in December 1960; triumphantly and officially achieved by Michael Ramsay to Paul VI March 1966; consolidated by Donald Coggan again to Paul VI in April 1977; and reversed by Robert Runcie when he invited John Paul II to Canterbury in May 1982.[36]

Significant among the meetings mentioned in the citation above was that of the Anglican/Roman Catholic International

---

34. See George Tavard, *The Thousand Faces of the Virgin Mary*, Collegeville MN: The Liturgical Press, 1996
35. Paul VI, *Marialis cultus*, Vatican: Vatican Polyglot Press, 1974, par 32
36. Alberic Stacpoole, 'Mary in Ecumenical Dialogue' in J. Hyland (ed), *Mary in the Church*, Dublin: Veritas, 1989, p 67

Commission (ARCIC). This is a body of Anglican and Catholic theologians established in 1966 by Paul VI and the then Archbishop of Canterbury, Michael Ramsey, to engage in, 'serious dialogue, which founded on the gospels and on the ancient common traditions, may lead to that unity in truth, for which Christ prayed'.[37] The continuing work of ARCIC is an attempt to find substantial agreement on controversial issues. In 1981, they agree, for example, on one Mediator between God and humankind who is Jesus Christ and they reject any interpretation of Mary's role which is other than this interpretation.[38] However, in the same document pertaining to the dogmas of the Immaculate Conception and the Assumption, agreement was more problematic, as seen in the following statement:

> ... the dogmas of the Immaculate Conception and the Assumption raise a special problem for those Anglicans who do not consider that the precise definitions given by these dogmas are sufficiently supported by scripture. For many Anglicans the teaching authority of the Bishop of Rome, independent of a council, is not recommended by the fact that through it these Marian doctrines were proclaimed as dogmas binding on all the faithful. Anglicans would also ask whether, in any future union between our two churches, they would be required to subscribe to such dogmatic statements. One consequence of our separation has been a tendency for Anglicans and Roman Catholics alike to exaggerate the importance of the Marian dogmas in themselves at the expense of other truths more closely related to the foundation of the Christian faith.[39]

Nonetheless from 2005, ARCIC was making some progress as witnessed in a commentary by the Pontifical Council for Promoting Christian Unity based on the, 'Seattle Statement

37. Anglican/Roman Catholic International Commission., J. Yarnold and H. Chadwick (eds), *An ARCIC Catechism*, London: Catholic Truth Society, 1983, p 1
38. Anglican/Roman Catholic Joint Preparatory Commission., 'Authority in the Church II' [online] http://www.prounione. urbe.-it/dia-int/arcic/doc/i_arcic_authority2.html [Accessed 31 October 2007].
39. Anglican/Roman Catholic Joint Preparatory Commission., 'Authority in the Church II' [online].

Anglican/Roman Catholic International Commission (ARCIC 11)'.[40] The Pontifical Council displays some level of optimism concerning the two Marian dogmas when it writes:

> Today ARCIC looks to a common re-reception of Marian doctrine ... the Commission expresses the hope that the two bodies can recognise in each other's convictions genuine expressions of Christian faith, even though the same formulations are not used, namely those of the definitions of 1854 and 1950, which, however, Anglicans would respect as legitimate.[41]

Aside from ARCIC, throughout the years many theologians from all beliefs and religious practices came together to work out varying kinds of joint declarations.[42] Authentic dialogue in shared research is evident particularly in the work of the Lutheran theologian Jürgen Moltmann. Writing frankly, he explains that Christian churches must make a greater effort to work towards an ecumenically compelling Marian theology. He had little qualms about saying that the history of Mary and her devotion has been far more divisive than unitive. He strongly believes that the greater the Marian superstructure became, the more divisive it has been for ecumenical relationships.[43] Moltmann envisages a viable ecumenical Marian theology, provided three criteria are met. Firstly, the source of Marian theology must be found in the scriptures in the biblical Miriam, Mary the mother of Jesus. Secondly, Marian theology must serve christology and not detract from it in any way. Thirdly, Moltmann believes that a biblically-based and Christocentric Marian theology, 'will express the presence and activity of the Holy Spirit in the destiny of Christ and all Christians'.[44]

40. See, for example, Jared Wicks, 'A Commentary on Mary: Grace and Hope in Christ of the Anglican-Roman Catholic International Com mis-sion, 2005' [online] http://www.vatican.va/roman_curia/ pontifical_councils/?chrstuni/angl-comm-docs/rc_ [Accessed 31 Oct 2007].
41. Wicks, 'A Commentary on Mary: Grace and Hope in Christ' [online].
42. Stefano de Fiores, 'Mary in Postconciliar Theology' in R. Latourelle (ed) *Vatican II Assessment and Perspectives* Vol. 1, New York: Paulist Press, 1988, p 489
43. Jurgen Moltmann, 'Editorial: Can there be an ecumenical Mariology'? *Concilium*, Vol 163, (1983), p XII.
44. Moltmann, 'Editorial', p XV

However, despite the efforts of Moltmann and those working towards ecumenism on all sides, real concerns are voiced today about the risk that these 'compromises' have imposed on Mary. Spretnak, for example, takes issue with the 'downplaying' of Mary's devotional role by the council in the interests of ecumenism. In the years subsequent to its closing, she believes that a great silence clouded the person and theology of one of the most important symbols that the Catholic Church has ever known. In her own words Spretnak counts herself:

> [A]mong an increasing, number of liberals who have developed a properly 'bad attitude' about the church's drastic reduction of Marian spirituality in our lifetime. The Roman Catholic Church is a container and guardian of mysteries far greater than itself. It had always recognised not only the biblical delineations of Mary, as do the Protestant and Orthodox branches of Christianity, but also what could be called the biblical*plus* perception of her, as do the Orthodox.[45]

She goes on to say that the Second Vatican Council fathers were correct in almost everything they did except for the, 'profoundly wrong decision about demoting Mary and shrinking her officially recognised presence to primarily being no more than an exemplary member of the church and a 'model' or cipher representing it in scripture'.[46] In this respect, she raises what she visualises is a key question as to why, after four-hundred and forty-years of Protestantism, was it so compelling for so many young Catholic European theologians and priests to adopt the rallying cry of 'ecumenism' at the Second Vatican Council? Furthermore, she wonders why, in the time frame between the 1950s and the Council in the 1960s, did so many Catholic men all of a sudden, 'agree with theological positions favouring a drastic diminution of Mary that previously would have been unthinkable'?[47]

Spretnak criticises the council by claiming that it cast a long and negative shadow over Marian hymns, devotions and the rosary, as they were largely phased out in parishes particularly

45. Spretnak, *Missing Mary*, p 3
46. Spretnak, *Missing Mary*, p 11
47. Spretnak, *Missing Mary*, p 11

in the States. These changes also included removal of her statues from many Catholic churches. Furthermore, research on Marian theology was somewhat adversely affected, at least symbolically, when one of the largest Marian libraries in the world, in Dayton, Ohio, was given an instruction to suspend three of its Marian publications. Its location was relegated from the wing adjoining the main campus library to a seventh-floor less high profile position for fear of impeding 'ecumenical dialogue'.[48] Furthermore, the loss experienced by those who had a high spiritual regard for Mary was inestimable. Poignantly Spretnak gives an account of a discussion with a colleague of like mind who tells her that, as a result of the church's diminishment of Mary's role in its devotion and liturgical practices, 'an entire spiritual, aesthetic culture was betrayed and destroyed'.[49] Perhaps the faithful who hold Mary and her importance in the church in very high regard will agree with Spretnak when she criticises those who frequently express the, 'assertion that the church is far better off for having deleted the Queen of Heaven'.[50]

As to why after several centuries it was so compelling to forsake Mary in the interests of ecumenism, and why the apparent sudden drastic diminution of her took place in the wake of the Second Vatican Council, is somewhat difficult to answer with certainty. If this is really what happened, it would not be too difficult to agree with Spretnak's interpretation of the situation. Those who treasure Mary as indispensable to their lives as Christians are undoubtedly grieving for the relative loss of the Mary they knew in the tradition. Perhaps the council and its concern for ecumenism, albeit with the greatest of intentions, is somewhat to blame. The heady days of pre-Vatican II mariology are gone and Catholic Christianity may have been robbed for all time of the Mary it knew. Perhaps also the price paid in the interests of ecumenism was too high. Was the relative loss of the only woman whose reputation survived completely unscathed in Catholic Christianity for two millennia worth it? Only time will tell.

---

48. Spretnak, *Missing Mary*, p 50
49. Spretnak, *Missing Mary*, p 50
50. Spretnak, *Missing Mary*, p 6

The Ecclesiatype Humanised

Did Mary indeed fall so far? Has she really disappeared? Few would be likely to agree that she has vanished into the abyss of nothingness. Among the millions of Catholics who know of her existence, doubtless there are those whose theatypical and christatypical approaches remain constant. In addition, for as long as the ecclesiatypical approach continues to exist, Mary will not be lost to Catholic Christianity. Furthermore, we can argue that the Second Vatican Council and ecumenical endeavours probably did more to emphasise the rightful understanding of Mary than heretofore. Specifically, they asked that her followers look to her humanity in the context of her status as a woman of the church communities. They endeavoured to defend that humanity in much the same way as did some of the early fathers and theologians mentioned at the beginning of this chapter – Ambrose, Ignatius, Epiphanius, Augustine and Chrysostom.

Mary as Ecclesiatype is, therefore, concomitant with her humanity. In this respect, Semmelroth made a significant contribution to our ecclesiological understanding of Mary where he was keenly attracted to Ambrose's tenet that Mary is a 'Type of the Church'. That principle is dear to Semmelroth, not only because it came from the early days of Christianity but also because he understood that it belongs to, 'the innermost and essential substance of Christian reality'.[51] He developed the theme by referring to Mary as Archetype of the church, pointing out that the church is made up of an invisible, spiritual core as well as a visible and tangible one. As Type of the church, Mary represents the church's nature, while her personal component brings the church closer to humanity.[52]

Just to draw a contrast, Vollert criticises a theology which places Mary closer to the church than to Christ. He reasons that the mystery of Mary finds its explanation only in Christ, the Incarnate Word. He believes she is closer to Christ than to the church since it is through her maternal relation with him that she receives her maternal relation with the church. Furthermore, her collaboration in building up the church is a natural

---

51. Semmelroth, *Mary the Archetype of the Church*, p 26
52. Semmelroth, *Mary the Archetype of the Church*, pp 30-32

consequence of her collaboration with Christ in the redemption of humankind.[53] Undoubtedly Vollert is christatypical in his Marian approach. Although Semmelroth, like Vollert, accepts the very great importance of Mary's motherhood, unlike Vollert, he believes that her motherhood cannot be the principle from which the rest of Marian theology derives.[54] If this were the case then he argues that, 'one is apt to find facile reasonings which cannot conceal a certain speciousness and superficiality'.[55] Mary is to be sought at the very centre of the work of salvation but only through her position as Archetype of the church. In this way of thinking then, Semmelroth emphasises that it is the *Ecclesia* and not Mary's motherhood which is at the heart of the economy of salvation.[56]

The following summary might now be useful with respect to accounting for the ecclesiatypical approach. Firstly, it is important to recognise the very important relationship between Mary and the church, with its roots in the early fathers. Secondly, a stronger emphasis is placed on Mary's ecclesiological role than on a christological one. Thirdly, we discover that Mary's role in salvation is not of itself Christ-centred but instead it is *ecclesia*-centred – a testimony which interprets the church as having a human face made tangible through Mary as Type of the church. Fourthly, we recognise how the Second Vatican Council's ecclesiology of Mary influences our understanding of Mary as Ecclesiatype. More is to be said, however. Since the time of the council, a considerable amount of official literature written about Mary has been penned by Paul VI and John Paul II. In the following two sections it will be shown that these two popes respectively reveal a strong ecclesiatypical orientation in their writings.

Paul VI: Mary as Ecclesiatype
There are ecclesiatypical themes running through one of the most important church documents on Mary subsequent to the

---

53. Cyril Vollert, *A Theology of Mary*, Herder and Herder: New York, 1965, p 46

54. Semmelroth, *Mary the Archetype of the Church*, pp 7-19

55. Semmelroth, *Mary the Archetype of the Church*, p 20

56. Semmelroth, *Mary the Archetype of the Church*, p 24

57. Paul VI, *Marialis cultus*, Vatican City: Vatican Polyglot Press, 1974

council, Paul VI's Apostolic Exhortation *Marialis cultus*.[57] The
publication of this document in 1974 ensured that the relative
Marian silence in the intervening years since the end of the
council in 1965 had now concluded. The Exhortation was
certainly welcome, making it clear that something of the utmost
importance to Catholic Christianity had not truly been lost,
despite Spretnak's conviction that, 'The Queen of Heaven was
deemed problematic by a hierarchy of powerful men who then
'disappeared' her former presence.'[58] It is difficult to accept that
Christ's mother was intended to be 'disappeared'. A closer look
at one of the council's phrases in *Lumen gentium* reads, 'this
sacred synod ... does not ... intend to give a complete doctrine
on Mary, nor does it wish to decide those questions which the
work of theologians has not yet fully clarified'.[59] What the
council in fact did was to leave the way open for further
theological research, a great deal of which has taken place in
Marian theology since those years with Paul VI taking the lead
on behalf of the magisterium. His task was to place Mary within
a proper context for Christian worship and, with this in mind,
he turned his attention to the key principles of Marian devotion
in relation to the liturgy, the church, the Trinity, the scriptures,
ecumenism and anthropology.

Following the directives of the council, Paul VI kept in mind
its guidelines on the *General Calendar*[60] for the celebration of the
mysteries of the faith throughout the liturgical year. In his
Apostolic Exhortation, therefore, prominence is given to the
work of salvation by ensuring that the primary focus of the
liturgical year is always on Christ but includes commem-
orations of Mary in the annual cycle of her Son's mysteries. He
communicates that 'this balance can be taken as a norm for
preventing any tendency (as has happened in certain forms of

---

58. Spretnak, *Missing Mary*, p 57

59. Vatican Council II, *Lumen gentium*, par 54

60. The Council had already ordered a revision of the General Calendar.
This task was undertaken by the Sacred Congregation for Divine
Worship in 1969, a version of which is to be found in Sacred
Congregation for Divine Worship, *General Norms for the Liturgical Year
and Calendar*, M. A. Simcoe (ed), Chicago: Liturgy Training
Publications, 1985, pp 179-195

popular piety) to separate devotion to the Blessed Virgin from its necessary point of reference – Christ'.[61] The Pope reminds the faithful that, just like the primitive church witnessed Mary as one who prays with the apostles, the modern church visualises her as 'actively present ... and ... desires to live the mystery of Christ with her'.[62] In this way, the papal document exhorts Mary as vital to the life of the church by firmly establishing her place among its peoples. Donal Flanagan reiterates this teaching when he interprets the main thrust of Paul VI's document as emphasising, 'clearly that the liturgical renewal has, indeed, given her full and proper place to Mary in the church's worship'.[63]

Nor are guidelines for private non-liturgical devotion to Mary overlooked in Paul VI's Exhortation, although he avoids making statements that would apply universally. He is quite conscious that devotion to Mary in the Catholic Church in Europe is very different to that, for example, of Latin America. In this regard, he encourages the local churches to work out their own criteria for devotion to Mary since they are best in tune with the needs of their respective peoples. Wisely the Pope advises, 'We would like this revision to be respectful of wholesome tradition and open to the legitimate requests of the people of our time.'[64] We may claim here that his Exhortation with respect to Mary as Ecclesiatype is palpable where he specifies: 'Marian devotion must always recognise the mysterious oneness which exists between Mary and the church community ... love for the church will become love for Mary, and vice versa, since the one cannot exist without the other'.[65]

Overall, what insights may we garner from *Marialis cultus*? Primarily with his intent on the right ordering of the liturgy, Paul VI draws a clear demarcation line between worship of God and the kind of devotion which is officially sanctioned for the Mother of God Incarnate. In addition, he permits Mary to be

---

61. Paul VI, *Marialis cultus*, par 17
62. Paul VI, *Marialis cultus*, par 11
63. Donal Flanagan, 'The Veneration of Mary: a New Papal Document', *The Furrow*, Vol 25, No 5 (1974), pp 272-277
64. Paul VI, *Marialis cultus*, par 24
65. Paul VI, *Marialis cultus*, par 28

recognised as a Type of the church, returning her to her full humanity among its peoples. Mary is thus imaged as a woman among women and a woman among men but not to be idolised as a goddess or a *Christus*; rather she is one who guides her followers to live out gospel values to the full. In this way, Pope Paul VI advises that she is not beyond the reach of those who wish to image her at their side – for she is, indeed, the Ecclesiatype.

John Paul II: Mary as Ecclesiatype

Now we turn to Paul VI's successor, Pope John Paul II where ecclesiatypical propensity is also evident in his work. The primary focus of this section is that of the last major Marian work to have been published by John Paul. In March 1987, he produced his Encyclical *Redemptoris mater* or *Mary Mother of the Redeemer*.[66] The Encyclical is the longest document ever to have been written by a pope on Mary to date. Its issue was intended to set the tone for the Marian Year (1987-1988) and it had a dual function.[67] Firstly, it was to serve as an outline of religious celebrations for that particular year, and secondly it was intended to offer official up-to-date teaching on Mary for that time.

The Marian theology of John Paul II, whether it is found in his official documents or in the Vatican press, contains many elements of Mary as Ecclesiatype. Overall it is being suggested here that John Paul's encyclical letter, like *Marialis Cultus*, is essentially ecclesiatypical in tone. This is evident from its very sub-title found in the text: 'The Blessed Virgin Mary in the Life of the Pilgrim Church', primarily linking Mary to the church. The letter deals with her, 'active and exemplary presence in the life of the church'[68] while at the same time emphasising that she cannot take the place of Christ as mediator between God and humankind. The document is, however, different in purpose to *Marialis cultus* since it is not particularly concerned with the

---

66. John Paul II, *Mary Mother of the Redeemer*, Dublin: Veritas, 1987
67. See Thomas O'Loughlin, *Marian Encyclical*, Dublin: Veritas, 1987, p 5. O'Loughlin explains that the background to the message of that Marian Year was significant for the approach of the second millennium. Since Mary preceded the birth of Christ at the beginning of the first millennium, the faithful should turn to her as they approach the second one.
68. John Paul II, *Mother of the Redeemer*, par 1

right ordering of devotion to Mary. Rather it is doctrinal. Perhaps John Paul II recognised that his predecessor had advised sufficiently about liturgical and devotional teaching as the following statement suggests:

> Shortly after the Council, my great predecessor Paul VI decided to speak further of the Blessed Virgin. In ... *Marialis Cultus* he expounded the foundations and criteria of the special veneration which the Mother of Christ receives in the church, as well as the various forms of Marian devotion – liturgical, popular, private ...[69]

The way was paved, therefore, for John Paul II to concentrate on doctrinal formulations where he employs both the scriptures and *Lumen gentium* to inform his Marian theology. *Redemptoris mater* contains fifty-two paragraphs, forty-two of which make reference to the scriptures. He is also concerned that the faithful continue to recognise the teaching of *Lumen gentium* where Mary is central to the life of the church. In that context, never again should she be relegated to the margins of an isolated mariology. Out of the fifty-or-so sections in his encyclical, John Paul makes approximately thirty-five statements directly relating Mary to the church. The christatypical title of Mary as Co-Redeemer is not directly adverted to in *Redemptoris mater*, rather her role as Mother of the Redeemer is emphasised as in the following quote: 'Mary became not only "nursing mother" of the Son of Man but also the "associate of unique mobility" of the Messiah and Redeemer.'[70] Neither does John Paul neglect some mention of Mary in relation to the Mediatrix question. Undoubtedly, he would be concerned about the centrality of Christ's unique position in reiterating the council's teaching, for he counsels that the, 'church knows and teaches with Saint Paul that, *"there is only one mediator"*.'[71]

In his personal Marian devotion, however, John Paul II tends to write with an enthusiasm and fondness symptomatic of one who has an especial relationship with the mother of Jesus. In the official Vatican *L'Osservatore Romano*, for example, he wrote an

---

69. John Paul II, *Mother of the Redeemer*, par 2
70. John Paul II, *Mother of the Redeemer*, par 39
71. John Paul II, *Mother of the Redeemer*, par 38

incredible amount of articles on Mary during the course of his pontificate.[72] In this newspaper, on an anniversary of the Lourdes apparitions, he prays with elated enthusiasm: 'Hail Mary ... Today I would like to be in Spirit in that corner of France where for a hundred and twenty one years these words have been murmured incessantly by the lips of thousands of millions of men and women ...'[73]

In accordance with his own personal consecration, evident from in his Marian motto *Totus Tuus*, this well travelled man entrusted each and every nation to the maternal care of the Blessed Virgin. Is this excessive? Was John Paul was attempting excessive elevation of Mary by reversing some of the teachings of chapter eight of *Lumen gentium* through his Marian devoutness? It is certainly unlikely and, in this respect, perhaps the opinion of Peter Hebblethwaite, writing during the early stages of John Paul's pontificate, is worth noting. Hebblethwaite interprets the Pontiff's exceptional devotion to Mary as something peculiar to the Pope himself rather than of any great significance to official church teaching. Although much of what John Paul was saying has been written in the Vatican's *L'Osservatore Romano*, it would not be taken generally as doctrinal or official church teaching, and what is contained therein would not have the same official standing in encyclicals such as *Redemptoris Mater*.[74]

Conclusion

As the chapter draws to a close, an underlying theme is emerging. This clearly stresses the importance of the ecclesiatypical approach as a way of imaging Mary from the perspective of her humanity and how she is present to the church as the People of

72. See John Paul II, 'At the Root of the Eucharist is the Virginal and Maternal Life of Mary', *L'Osservatore Romano*, Vol 24, No 788 (1983), pp 11-12; John Paul II, 'Mary is the Greatest Success of the Paschal Mystery', *L'Osservatore Romano*, Vol 17, No 781 (1983), p 2; John Paul II, 'Uphold Dignity of Motherhood', *L'Osservatore Romano*, Vol 3, No 564 (1979), pp 1-9
73. John Paul II, 'The Magnificat Answers Questions on Evangelizing, *L'Osservatore Romano*, Vol 9, No 950 (1979), p 3
74. Peter Hebblethwaite, 'The Mariology of Three Popes', *The Way*, Vol 51 (1984), pp 63-67

God. We understand what it means to be human. Insofar as we are Christians, we also experience what it means to be church, secure in the knowledge that Mary best relates to us in a tangible way through the universal medium of the *Ecclesia*. This low mariology is not to deny the significance of some elements of either the theatypical or christatypical approaches in the previous chapters, for they contain various components central to the Marian dogmas, doctrines and important symbolism. These include, for example, her *Theotokos* title, her Immaculate Conception and her assumption. Specifically, however, Mary as Ecclesiatype is a way of relating to Mary primarily through her earthly attributes without dismissing the core teaching, representations and imagery that have accrued around her person. We are human, Mary is human. We are able to access her humanity and she is able to access our humanity. A pattern of relationship thus emerges, promoting companionship between Mary and the church as the People of God where the primary emphasis rests within the context of her human nature – a fact that has not been lost to Catholic teaching.

We are able to say, therefore, with a degree of confidence that the basis of Mary as Ecclesiatype may be gleaned from some of the earliest writers such as Ignatius, Epiphanius, Chrysostom, Augustine and Ambrose. Fifteen-hundred years later, in our own times, attention to Mary's unique relationship with the church, primarily through her humanity, remains staunchly within our grasp. Specifically we recognise that understanding in certain documents of the magisterium, particularly in chapter eight of *Lumen gentium* and in the writings of Pope Paul VI and John Paul II. Although sensitivity to ecumenism was of the utmost importance, the council made it abundantly clear that Mary and the church were inseparable, a truth to be found especially in the ecclesiological emphasis of that particular document. In recognition of this teaching, Paul VI set about contextualising devotion to Mary, not just in relation to the Trinity, liturgy and ecumenism, but also by stressing her place in the milieu of the scriptures, the church and anthropology. John Paul II followed with doctrinal formulae depending on the scriptures and *Lumen gentium* to inform his Marian theology.

CHAPTER FOUR

I am Woman

The People's Mary

The presentation of Mary as Ecclesiatype in chapter eight of *Lumen gentium,* and in the writings of Pope Paul VI and John Paul II disclose the robust portrait of a woman aware of her own personal vocation. In the same way, Mary also symbolises for us the fundamental vocation of the church community where we discover her in the complexity of our Christian faith. We learn from her the ideals of Christian living through the 'bits and pieces' of our everyday mortal lives. It is possible to contend then that to identify with Mary is to understand the church, for she is the people's Mary. Of course coming fully to terms with the meaning of church is an extravagant claim and not possible beyond the bounds of human reason, which brings us to the point of this chapter. Turning to the presentation of Mary as a Type for the Church means questioning seriously just what sort of church that is – for all has not always been well in its long history. Nor is it authentic simply to select the positive aspects of being a member of the church without admitting of the injustices that took place against the People of God from within.

Some of the injustices were perpetrated particularly against women and any solid history of Christian feminist theology will testify to such a claim.[1] It is not within the remit of this chapter to offer a feminist interpretation of ecclesiastical chronicles about the relationship between the church and women. Nonetheless, it would be remiss not to dedicate a little space to ongoing challenges with reference to the substantive issue of women's place in the church. By way of association, we include

---

1. See Mary T Malone, *Women and Christianity: The First Thousand Years,* Vol 1, Dublin: The Columba Press, 2000; *Women and Christianity: The Medieval Period AD 1000-1500,* Vol 2, Dublin: The Columba Press, 2001; *Women and Christianity: From the Reformation to the 21st Century,* Vol 3, Dublin: The Columba Press, 2003

the experience of the people's Mary as one among her own sex
who has often been imaged in a way that she could never have
possibly desired. Conscientious Christian women are not likely
to accept, in the words of Jo Ann Kay McNamara, a 'Mary [who]
became a consolidated stereotype of feminine virtue
comfortably ensconced in heaven and exquisitely malleable to
monkish visions and fantasies'.[2] Although McNamara is
making reference to a patriarchal understanding of Mary in
medieval times, it is one that would have been held by many for
hundreds of years before and after that period. Habitually Mary
has been used to secure patriarchal social structures, often at the
expense of women serving to lower their status through time
immemorial.

Christopher O'Donnell advises, however, that there is another
important way of discovering Mary. In particular he refers to
the exhortations of Paul VI and John Paul II (*Marialis Cultus* and
Redemptoris Mater) to account for the significance of women who
write about Mary. Regardless of whether they are mothers, widows,
celibate or married, women possess a lens through which Mary can
be reflected. O'Donnell suggests that an inclusive model for all can
be found in her with the help of feminist and other women writers
leading to her deeper understanding. A discovery, therefore, is to
be made in particular through:

> ... women writing on Mary within the broad tradition of
> mariology. We also have theologians more explicitly
> feminist. These latter are acutely aware of the past flaws in
> male representations of Mary. It is not very helpful,
> however, to see in the history of marian theology and piety a
> deliberate ploy to distract women by means of Mary, and so
> keep them in subjugation to a patriarchal church.[3]

It is clear that O'Donnell is very aware of the difficult
situation in which many women in the church have found
themselves throughout the centuries. This is obvious from his
reference to the misuse of Mary, where at times in the tradition

---

2. Jo Ann Kay McNamara., *Sisters in Arms*, Massachusetts: Harvard
University Press, 1992
3. Christopher O'Donnell, *At Worship With Mary*, Delaware: Michael
Glazier, 1988, pp 168-169

she has been used as a tool of subjugation to keep women in a
lesser place than men. Nonetheless he is hopeful that from out of
the patriarchal culture feminist and other women writers will
'render the church'[4] a service through the benefit of their own
particular perspectives.

The next and final chapter will introduce some of those
theologians to show that this challenge has been met to a certain
extent with reference to Mary. It will also serve as a means of
developing Mary as Ecclesiatype with allusion to how that
particular approach, or way of imaging her, has the wherewithal
to act as a theology common both to church teaching and to
Christian feminism. In the meantime some of the problems with
patriarchy and the difficulties that women in the church have
encountered are worthy of examination.

Resident Aliens

The story of women in Christianity is not easily told. Elizabeth
Schüssler Fiorenza bears witness to that complex saga by
referring to women as 'resident aliens' when she claims that
they are relegated to a position of subservience in their
respective church institutions. According to her reckoning, many
women find themselves in a somewhat anomalous situation
since they are both inside and outside these institutions at one
and the same time. They are inside due to their continued
affiliation and loyalty, but they are outside in terms of language,
experience, culture and history. Hierarchical organisations,
Schüssler Fiorenza believes, are responsible for putting women
into this position by silencing them and excluding them from
institutional leadership ranks.[5]

Katie Cannon is of a mind with Schüssler Fiorenza when,
writing recently, she suggests that contemporary women will
get sick and tired of their sexuality being looked upon as
something of a curse rather than a blessing. Although she also
questions central aspects of Christianity, she willingly remains
within the tradition calling for others not to give up wrestling

---

4. O'Donnell, *At Worship With Mary*, p 169
5. Elizabeth Schüssler Fiorenza, 'Feminist studies in religion and a radical democratic ethos' [online] http://www.unisa.ac.za/default.asp?
Cmd=ViewContent&ContentID=7347 [Accessed 24 June 2007]

with the difficult questions until the situation has improved.[6] It is the job, therefore, of feminist theology, and Christian feminist theology in particular, to enable women to contribute to the creation of emancipating structures within their own faith communities. In addition, it is the business of feminist theologians to articulate, reinterpret and re-categorise the layers of interpretation provided by the sacred scriptures, tradition, history and the social constructs of their respective faiths and religions.[7]

The following quotation from the American exegete Sandra Schneiders will suffice to set the tone and summarise some examples of the situation as it is often perceived by feminist theologians:

> What is one to do when the male God-Image that nourished one's faith from infancy to adulthood becomes at best incredible and at worst oppressive? How is one to relate to a male saviour who represents a male God who is invoked to legitimate the claim that maleness is normative for humanity? Where does one turn when sacraments have ceased to mediate the encounter with God because they are experienced as instruments for a sacralised subjugation of women believers by male clerics? What does one do with the endless and exhausting rage that is called forth by sexual apartheid in the church, by ubiquitous linguistic sexism, by clerical monopoly of ministry, by blatantly oppressive liturgy?[8]

Ultimately, the difficulties arising from these issues will take a great deal of effort, on both the part of the church authorities and of Christian feminists, to resolve. Neither for these women nor for the leaders of the church can the abandonment of the institution wherein they each practise their faith ever be countenanced. Nonetheless, the problem will not just disappear. We cannot pretend that either side exclusively holds the answers. Furthermore, no amount of justified anger on the part

---

6. Katie Cannon, 'Erotic Justice: Authority, Resistance, and Transformation', *Journal of Feminist Studies in Religion*, Vol 23, No 1 (2007), p 25
7. Elizabeth Schzüssler Fiorenza, 'Feminist studies in religion and a radical democratic ethos' [online].
8. Sandra Schneiders, *Beyond Patching*, New York: Paulist Press, 1991, p 3

of Christian feminism, or authoritative documentation from the magisterium, will resolve the difficulties unless substantial agreement is found. That is why we must recognise, with blunt honesty and humility, the nature of some of the gender issues which threaten to weaken Christ's church on earth.

Feminism vs Patriarchy

The situation becomes more convoluted when we appreciate that, from the middle of the twentieth-century until today, it is generally agreed that feminism does not constitute a static and monolithic intellectual or political project, specifically because women are not all the same.[9] Any definition which attempts to encapsulate the meaning of feminism runs the risk of being misconstrued through too narrow a classification of the term where explication is attempted. In fact, some writers use the term 'feminisms' to express the many interpretations of this complex ideology. Since such is the case, it is judicious to offer at least one designation. In this respect, Schneiders is succinct:

> Feminism, I would propose, is a comprehensive ideology which is rooted in women's experience of sexual oppression, engages in a critique of patriarchy as an essentially dysfunctional system, embraces an alternative vision for humanity and the earth, and actively seeks to bring this vision to realisation.[10]

We distinguish here the many possible forms of feminisms' 'comprehensive ideology' which is applicable both to secular and to religious patriarchy. Within the ideology of the secular, its aspects include liberal feminism, cultural feminism, socialist feminism and radical feminism.[11] Linda Hogan would concur that:

> The relationship between women's experience and feminist theory is a complex one. Women's experience is a central resource certainly ... but it requires interpretation and critique.

---

9. Margaret Miles, 'Roundtable Discussion Feminist Religious History', *Journal of Feminist Studies in Religion*, Vol 22, No 1 (2006), p 53
10. Schneiders, *Beyond Patching*, p 15
11. Schneiders, *Beyond Patching*, pp 15-25

Feminists must be able to acknowledge and arbitrate among competing subjectivities, since women do not share a uniform experience or material reality.[12]

Patriarchy, for its part, is about the structuring of society on the basis of family units wherein fathers or other males have primary responsibility for the welfare of these units. The concept of patriarchy often refers to the expectation that men take primary responsibility for the welfare of the community as a whole, acting as representatives via public office. Of itself, it cohabits comfortably with a certain malaise evident in every age, class and culture, permitting not only the marginalisation of women but a belief in their inferior status. Throughout the centuries, it has divided and separated men and women, controlling how they think and behave for fear of threat to the so-called dominant order. As Ruether advises, a gender dualism based on sexism[13] brought into effect by patriarchy, is dangerous to the welfare of humankind because it places a greater value on one member of the pair, correspondingly subordinating its opposite member.[14] It may then be possible to refer to other dualisms sometimes at play. For example, the body is divided from the soul and is inferior to it, the universe is inferior to heaven and is separated from it, and white middle class males are the ideal model for humankind, where the female counter-part and all other races are inferior to the male. If these are the eyes through which we look at the world, then Ruether believes that we fall short of the divine plan of the Creator.[15]

12. Linda Hogan., *From Women's Experience to Feminist Theology*, Sheffield: Sheffield Academic Press, 1995, p 17

13. See Rosemary Ruether, 'The Interrelatedness of Oppression and Efforts for Liberation: A Feminist Perspective' in V. Fabella and S. Torres (eds), *Doing Theology in a Divided World*, New York: Orbis Books, 1985, p 65. Ruether explains that sexism is a corollary of patriarchy. Man must stop imaging himself as the superior being, but equally woman must take responsibility for her role and function in the world by not trading her humanity for dependent forms of security.

14. Rosemary Ruether, *Sexism and God-Talk*, London: SCM Press, 1983. pp.173-175

15. Katherine Allen Rabuzzi, 'The Socialist Feminist Vision of Rosemary Radford Ruether', *Religious Studies Review*, Vol 15, No 1 (1989), p 6

Patriarchy's strongest opponent is radical feminism which, according to Schneiders, is perhaps the most critical of all feminist approaches. She reasons that radical feminism, particularly in Catholicism, 'is actually quite well founded' because the 'Roman Catholic Church, as a social institution, is perhaps the most patriarchal structure in the western world and it has, even at times, defined itself as hierarchical by divine institution'.[16] It is for this reason that: 'Catholic radical feminists have identified patriarchy in general and hierarchy (i.e. sacralised patriarchy) in particular as an irredeemably sinful structure whose transform-ation is demanded by the gospel and is the *sine qua non* of the coming of the reign of God which is, by divine institution, not a hierarchy but a discipleship of equals.'[17]

At a time in the church's history, with so many achievements in both ecumenism and inter-religious dialogue among non-members, it is unacceptable that we cannot be at one among ourselves to build and strengthen the Reign of God ostensibly because of gender issues.[18] Schüssler Fiorenza, indeed, expresses her belief that the term 'feminist' often brings with it emotional constraints and negative connotations. Such is the situation despite the fact that something in the region of 90 per cent of women polled in North America and Europe claim they have benefited from the aims of women's movements. At the same time, however, 70 per cent refuse to identify themselves as feminists lest they be perceived as biased, fanatical or man-haters. As a consequence, support for feminism in general has experienced a severe backlash and in particular in mainstream Christianity.[19]

---

16. Schneiders, *Beyond Patching*, pp 24-25
17. Schneiders, *Beyond Patching*, p 25
18. See Kathleen McPhillips, 'Speaking Out Gathering Women in the Postcolonial Pacific Region', *Journal of Feminist Studies in Religion*, Vol 23, No 1 (2007), p 118. According to McPhillips only small groups are left struggling to keep the voice of gender equality alive in their church-es. Indeed, the women's situation appears to be regressing in certain Christian environments. In particular, she is referring to the church of the Anglican Communion where the Sydney Church failed to get the question of women's ordination on to a synod agenda.
19. Elizabeth Schussler Fiorenza, 'Feminist studies in religion and a radical democratic ethos' [online].

One serious question must be raised. Is Christianity irredeemably patriarchal? Two authors who have left their respective Christian faith traditions, Mary Daly and Daphne Hampson, think so. Both Daly[20] and Hampson[21] deem that patriarchy adversely influenced the teachings of Christ to the extent that his true meaning and values have been lost forever. Daly is of the opinion that portraying Christ as the saviour of women is pointless because of the Christian emphasis on the maleness of Jesus. She refers to the worship of Jesus as tantamount to christolatry, where the strength of his male symbols has alienated and subordinated women, no longer permitting them to function effectively in Christianity.[22] Hampson, for her part, argues that attempting to uphold Christ's 'message' only circumvents the real problem, since the personhood of Jesus remains the central symbol for the institutional church. They believe that abandonment of the Christian institutional churches is the only solution for women since they cannot attain full humanity as long as they remain trapped in the patriarchal dependency of those structures.[23] Patriarchal Christianity betrays women, Hampson continues, because it requires humans to submit to the overarching will of a patriarchal deity symbolised in the personhood of Jesus. Besides, she wonders what the point of a message is anyway. Anyone can live the message of Jesus without having to be a Christian, and anyone can live independently of the person who holds it. If the perspectives of women like Daly and Hampson are justified, it is timely to ask what evidence there is for such attitudes.

20. Mary Daly, *The Church and the Second Sex*, London: Geoffrey Chapman, 1968. Daly is a former Catholic.
21. Daphne Hampson, *Theology and Feminism*, Massachusetts: Basil Blackwell, 1990. Hampson is a former Scottish Episcopalian.
22. Mary Daly, *Beyond God the Father*, Boston: Beacon Press, 1973, pp 13-63, 44-68, 69-71
23. Hampson, *Theology and Feminism*, pp 215-225. Although Hampson claims there can be no incompatibility between feminism and being religious, there is incompatibility between being feminist and being Christian.

Christian Feminism and Patriarchy

Let us commence with an example from the Hebrew scriptures. At the very beginning of the Bible we find that part of Genesis which recounts, through mythical allegory, the creation of the human race. The Revised Standard Version Catholic Edition reads: 'So God created man in his own image, in the image of God he created him; male and female he created them' (Gen 1:27). The equal nature of men and women in this verse is obvious. Nonetheless, it was less used and even virtually ignored in favour of the second Book of Genesis which says: 'then the Lord God formed man of dust from the ground, and breathed into his nostrils the breath of life; and man became a living being' (Gen 2:7). Eve comes later in that text with the following reference: 'So the Lord God caused a deep sleep to fall upon the man, and while he slept took one of his ribs and closed up its place with flesh; and the rib which the Lord God had taken from the man he made into a woman and brought her to the man' (Gen 2:21-22). By the time we arrive at the third Book of Genesis, Eve has caused some trouble for she tempted her partner in the following way:

> Now the serpent was more subtle than any other wild creature that the Lord God had made. He said to the woman, 'Did God say, "you shall not eat of any tree of the garden"?' And the woman said to the serpent, 'We may eat of the fruit of the trees of the garden; but God said, "You shall not eat of the fruit of the tree which is in the midst of the garden, neither shall you touch it, lest you die"' (Gen 3:1-4).

It is well known, of course, that the woman partook of the forbidden fruit then offered it to the man who ate it and they both hid from God because of their disobedient shame. Claire Murphy, accounting for these stories in chapters two and three of Genesis, sustains the argument that Eve was held responsible for 'The Fall' and became subject to her husband, thus projecting this subservience on to all women of future generations. Between the second and fifth centuries, the Genesis 2 and 3 passages influenced the fathers of the church to the extent that women were often condemned as wicked temptresses. Where this belief was upheld or sustained, the teachings of Jesus and his attitude towards women in the New Testament was not to the fore in certain prevailing patriarchal influences of the early fathers and subsequent theological writers. Even as the young Christian communities were developing, Murphy claims that throughout the history of Christianity the values of the gospel and those of the church with reference to women were often at odds. Certainly by the middle of the twentieth-century, feminist scholars were alerting their respective faith traditions to the influence of patriarchy and how its structures had manipulated church and society through improper hermeneutic exegesis.[24]

Patriarchy, as it is described above, is insidious if it attempts to interpret the teachings of Christ from an anti-female stance. Ruether would hold that christology itself has often been misinterpreted and used against women to keep them in a subjugated position.[25] God came more and more to be imaged as one whose revelations were for *his* sons and it was this class of humanity that *he* directly addressed. *His* sons became *his* responsible partners. A God-male-female hierarchy was set up in the Christian tradition, where women were expected to relate to men in much the same way that men were to relate to God.[26] Ruether goes on to say that if the male represents the fullness of the human potential, then the female, the second sex, must in some way be defective in body, mind and soul – a fate inherited by woman since 'The Fall'. Female confinement to a subservient position in the social order proves that the incarnation of the *Logos* of God into male form was not a historical accident. It was, rather, an ontological necessity. For this reason, the wholeness of human truth is represented in the male who in turn must be seen as head of the woman – a theme to be found, for example, in 1 Tim 2:11-15 which says: 'I permit no woman to teach or have authority over men; she is to keep silent. For Adam was formed first, then Eve; and Adam was not deceived, but the woman was deceived and became a transgressor'. Given that situation, women can never represent headship either in society or in the church.[27]

24. Claire Murphy, *Woman as Church*, Dublin: Gill & Macmillan, 1997, pp 3-6
25. Rosemary Ruether, *To Change the World*, London: SCM, 1981, p 45
26. Ruether, *Sexism*, pp 53-55.
27. Ruether, *To Change the World*, p 45

Mary Hembrow Snyder goes so far as to say that the lordship
of Christ was no longer permitted to liberate those who were
most vulnerable in society such as women, slaves and
conquered peoples. The dominators claimed that they derived
their lordship from Christ himself and justified their behaviour
as the norm for Christian living.[28] The maleness of the historical
Jesus undoubtedly reinforced this preference for male-identified
metaphors such as *Logos* and 'Son of God' over the lesser used
female metaphor *Sophia*.[29] This conception of christology
continued in the Greek and Hellenist Jewish tradition where
these patriarchal cultures developed the terms *Logos* and Christ,
according to their own androcentric bias. This culminated in a
firm belief that if Christ is male then the God he images must
also be male. Androcentric bias subsequently became part of the
Christian tradition where divinity, rationality and sovereign
power were all assumed to be male.[30]

If patriarchy has thus influenced Christianity to the extent
that women have been persistently denigrated or relegated to
inferior positions because of their sex, then undoubtedly the
potential for Christ's teachings have been thwarted. Can it be
contested, however, that patriarchal structures existing in the
church have denied and denigrated women? Certainly this is
evident if one is to accept Schneider's account above that the
church has displayed sexual apartheid, denies women the right
to mediate the sacraments or to represent Christ at the altar. It is
even more disconcerting if the male metaphor is seen solely as
the only appropriate one for God, with female metaphors either
being denied an equal place or virtually submerged in the
tradition. The primary contentious chestnut to be grappled with
in respect of patriarchal influence and women in Catholic
Christianity, however, is the vexed dispute about the mediation
of the sacraments.

---

28. Mary Hembrow Snyder, *The Christology of Rosemary Radford Ruether*,
Connecticut: Twenty Third Publications, 1988
29. Rosemary Ruether, 'Can Christology be Liberated from Patriarchy?'
in M. Stevens (ed), *Reconstructing the Christ Symbol: Essays in Feminist
Christology*, New York: Paulist Press, 1993, p. 7
30. Hembrow Snyder, *The Christology of Rosemary Radford Ruether*, pp
61-62

The Stained Glass Ceiling

One of the most contentious issues that the church and its members have continually had to encounter for sustained periods is the debate surrounding the inaccessibility of women to the ordained ministry.[31] It is difficult to see how the issue of women's ordination is unrelated to patriarchal structures. Whether members of the church like it or not, whatever the official teaching or whatever other views are expressed, this is a very real problem and there is little evidence to suggest that the questions it raises will become any less significant in the foreseeable future.[32] As Susan Ross puts it:

> The question of women's ordination is at the centre of any consideration of women in the church and its liturgical life. There is some evidence that women were ordained for certain functions in early and medieval Christianity. In modern Christianity, the issue of women's liturgical leadership has emerged as a consequence of arguments for women's equality. Nevertheless, it is important to note that questions about women's leadership and/or ordination have been raised since the beginning of Christianity and have been treated seriously by thinkers such as Thomas Aquinas.[33]

Catholicism is still in the throes of that thorny question because of widely varying truth claims on the matter. On the one hand, we have church teaching documenting five primary

---

31. Stephen Bates, 'The Stained-Glass Ceiling', *The Tablet*, Vol 28, (2004), pp 4-5. The term 'stained glass ceiling' refers to women's inability to gain senior positions in church institutions.

32. See Michael Maher, 'A Break with Tradition: Ordaining Women Rabbis, *Irish Theological Quarterly*, Vol 72, (2007), pp 32-43. This question does not arise for Catholicism in isolation from other faith traditions associated with Catholic Christianity. According to Maher, women's reform groups in America debate the ordination of women in the Protestant tradition. In Judaism, at a conference of over one thousand delegates in 1963, a proposal was put forward to resolve the matter. This did not happen until 1972 after many years of debate and counter-debate where the Reform branch of Judaism ordained its first woman rabbi.

33. Susan A. Ross, 'Church and sacrament – community and worship' in S. F. Parsons (ed), *The Cambridge Companion to Feminist Theology*, Cambridge: CUP, 2002, p 229

reasons for its position[34] and on the other hand, we have Christian feminist opponents challenging it.[35] The arguments considered to be the most important, according to the Sacred Congregation for the Doctrine of the Faith, against women taking Holy Orders are recorded in their document *Inter insigniores*. These are (i) the church's desire to be faithful to tradition (ii) Jesus did not call women to be a part of The Twelve (iii) and the priest acts *in persona Christi*.[36]

Church teaching has always proved to be unyielding on the ordination of women by relying in particular on the above rationale. Equally unyielding are the typical feminist responses in a number of familiar rebuttals. Firstly, where the church authorities maintain that they must be 'faithful to tradition', Christian feminists argue that reliance on precedence is not tenable given the critique of patriarchy and the unacceptable position in which women have been placed throughout that tradition. Secondly, although official teaching tells us that Jesus only called twelve men according to the synoptic gospels, Christian feminists are at pains to know who 'The Twelve' were exactly.[37] Matthew (10:1-4) and Mark (4:13-19) share the same names in that they count Thaddeus among their number but they both differ to Luke and Acts. Luke (6:12-16) and Acts (1:12-23) unlike Matthew and Mark include Judas Son of James in their account of the men who were called by Jesus. The number 'twelve' then is not about actual headcount; rather it is used in

34. See Richard McBrien, *Catholicism*, San Francisco: Harper San Francisco, 1994, p 778. McBrien outlines five main points of the church's teaching; (1) the tradition of Roman Catholicism has consistently opposed women's ordination, (2) Jesus did not call women, not even his own mother, to the priesthood, (3) an ordained priest must act in the name of Christ, and therefore must be a physical as well as a spiritual representation, (4) no one has a right to ordination, (5) women who were called deaconesses in the New Testament may not have been ordained.
35. See Carmel McEnroy, *Guests in Their Own House*, The Crossroad Publishing Company, New York: 1996; Mary Collins, 'The Refusal of Women in Clerical Circles' in M. Kolbenschlag (ed), *Women in the Church*, Washington DC: The Pastoral Press, 1987, pp 51-63
36. See Sacred Congregation for the Doctrine of the Faith, *Inter insigniores*, Catholic Truth Society: London, 1976
37. Rosemary Ruether, 'Male Clericalism and the Dread of Women', *Ecumenist*, Vol 11, No 5 (1973), p 65

the scriptures as symbolic of the ancient Twelve Tribes of Israel. By the time of Jesus, there were only two and a half tribes remaining. Confusion also revolves around the term 'apostles'. Paul and Barnabas were not part of 'The Twelve' but they were referred to as 'apostles'. In later tradition, Mary Magdalene became known as 'The apostle of the apostles' but like Paul and Barnabas she was not among 'The Twelve' called by Jesus. Given the above, it is thus not difficult to see why Christian feminists are not prepared to accept the argument that because Jesus called 'twelve men', women should be forbidden the sacrament of Holy Orders.

Official Church teaching places even greater importance on the third argument – the priest acts *in persona Christi*. The phrase is used to illustrate that only men can represent Christ at the Eucharist. As the Sacred Congregation for the Doctrine of the Faith teaches:

> The priest, alone who has the power to perform it, (i.e. the Eucharist) then acts not only through the effective power conferred on him by Christ, but *in persona Christi*, taking the role of Christ, to the point of being *his very image* (emphasis added) when he announces the words of consecration.[38]

The Congregation goes on to say that the faithful must be able to recognise easily that natural resemblance which exists between Christ and his priest. If the priest were female, it would be difficult to see in the minister the image of Christ.[39] According to this teaching, it is the physical appearance of the male which becomes the priority. Here the institution of an all-male priesthood has its explanation rooted in Christ's very maleness and it is the male which is the more accurate symbol. Put simply, Kenneth Untener explains that the term *in persona Christi* is relatively new in official documentation, evolving from an incorrect translation by Jerome (AD 347-420). The phrase, used apparently only once in the New Testament, is based on a faulty rendering of the original Greek. In 2 Corinthians 2:10, Paul writes '[what] I have forgiven, if I have forgiven anything, has been for your sake in the presence of Christ'. Jerome translated

---

38. Sacred Congregation, *Inter insigniores*, par 5
39. Sacred Congregation, *Inter insigniores*, par 5

this into Latin incorrectly substituting the word 'person' for the word 'presence'.[40] The phrase was seldom used again throughout the centuries until it was taken up by Pius XII in the twentieth-century where he proclaims:

> Now the minister, by reason of the sacerdotal consecration which he has received, is made like to the High Priest and possesses the power of performing actions in virtue of *Christ's very person* (emphasis added). Wherefore in his priestly activity he in a certain manner 'lends his tongue, and gives his hand' to Christ.[41]

The Second Vatican Council also makes explicit reference to the phrase a number of times when treating of the ordained priesthood.[42] This practice becomes increasingly common subsequent to the Council in the writings of Paul VI,[43] in the 1973 *General Instruction on the Roman Missal*[44] and in the 1971 Synod of Bishops, but without scholarly reference attaching to it.[45] The Congregation for the Doctrine of the Faith began to use it in 1973 and has frequently continued to do so.[46] Perhaps given the above accounts of how the term *in persona Christi* came about and its sparse usage for centuries, it is somewhat disingenuous

40. Kenneth Untener, 'Forum: The Ordination of Women. Can Horizons Widen'? *Worship*, Vol 65. No 1 (1991), p 53
41. Pius XII, '*Mediator Dei*, Encyclical of Pope Pius XII on the Sacred Liturgy …' http://www.vatican.va/holy_father/pius_xii/encyclicals/documents/hf_p-xii_enc_20111947_mediator-dei_en.html [Accessed 23 July 2007]
42. See Vatican Council II, *Sacrosanctum concilium*
43. Paul VI, 'Declaration On The Question Of Admission Of Women To The Ministerial Priesthood' http://www.papalencyclicals.net/Paul06/index.htm [Accessed 28 September 2007].
44. Congregation for Divine Worship., 'Defending the Faith' [online] http://www.cfpeople.org/Books/GIRM/GIRMp11.htm [Accessed 29 September 2007].
45. See Synod of Bishops, *Theology of Justice in the World 3*, Vatican City: Pontifical Biblical Commission for Justice and Peace, 1971. The 1971 Synod of Bishops was the Second General Assembly ever of the Synod of Bishops. Two matters for debate were on its agenda: i) The Ministerial Priesthood, ii) Justice in the World. Although it is better remembered for its latter document, it dealt with the former topic at length in its early meetings.
46. Untener, 'Forum', pp 55-59

to claim that only a male can represent Christ on the altar. As Osiek remarks, 'to say that Christ cannot be imaged as a woman is to say that woman cannot image Christ – this time not only as a priest, but not even as the crucified'.[47]

Remaining Within

'Why do women stay?' asks Fran Porter. It is a legitimate question for which she readily volunteers a rhetorical response – that is, despite the effort they experience with certain traditions and teachings, women embody a reality of faith which cannot be easily dismissed.[48] The truth of Christian faith must not be left behind regardless of the loneliness or struggle experienced by those who remain within the institution.[49] Faith in Christ is what matters and if one path to that faith is taken along the conduit of liberating feminist analysis, it is a better option than simply walking away. This is a courageous route and those who remain within the church will be better placed to put forward liberating challenges that have the potential to bring about revitalising change. Christian feminists are aware that Christianity and its earthly institutions do not have to be lost or repudiated in order to move forward. Instead, Christianity can strive to become evermore transformative through the liberating Christ who is above all human institutions. No Christian is to be separated from Christ and his message with respect to the coming of the Reign of God. In that context, Richard Clarke points out that, 'The only reasonable response by the church is to make certain that its "rules" are coherent and convincing rather than merely the fruits of its intrinsic authority'.[50]

Major attempts to introduce liberating change and create a more inclusive church community began with the work of the Second Vatican Council in the years 1962-1965. Since that time,

---

47. Carolyn Osiek, *Beyond Anger*, Dublin: Gill and Macmillan, 1986, p 71
48. Fran Porter, *It Will Not Be Taken Away From Her*, London: DLT, 2004, p 1
49. See Carol Christ and Judith Plaskow, *Womanspirit Rising: A Feminist Reading in Religion*, San Francisco: Harper and Row, 1979. Christ and Plaskow also claim women abandon their faith traditions because there is little hope of reform taking place in their lifetime.
50. Richard Clarke, *A Whisper of God*, Dublin: the Columba Press, 2006, p 50

Christian feminists have been able to hold out great hope with the onset of a new consciousness released by the council and which we now know can never be retracted. The efforts made were genuine and far superior to anything that had been previously attempted. Although the church was authoritative at the time of the council, it was nonetheless prophetic. So what was it about Vatican Council II that offered the hope which had eluded countless numbers of the faithful for centuries? Great tomes have been written since its opening but, put simply, Oliver Treanor explains that there are certain characteristics which differentiate it from former councils. Primarily the Second Vatican Council saw itself as pastoral. This was novel for a council which was set up not to react polemically against heresies but instead to minister exclusively to its people in the coming decades. Secondly, it was consciously christological and thirdly it was specifically ecclesiological.[51]

The time was now approaching for greater numbers of Catholic women to study scripture and tradition at doctoral level in the church's scholarly institutions. They were gaining the opportunity of academic employment – formerly permitted only to men. Eventually, young girls began to take their place among boys serving on the altar, women stood beside men to deliver the scriptural readings at Mass, the use of exclusive language in the liturgies began to disappear and the sex of the individual in the church community was of no consequence for the distribution of the sacred host. The Second Vatican Council promised liberating and transformative change for all women and men who were within. It became ever clearer that there is no reason to believe one must be either Christian or feminist, pro-male or pro-female, pro-humankind or pro-nature. As Letty Russell expresses it: 'It is both possible and necessary to be an advocate of more than one thing at a time. The world is not made up of either/ors ... [but it is] ... full of both/ands and maybe/alsos.'[52]

---

51. Oliver Treanor, *Mary Mother of the Redeemer, Mother of the Redeemed*, Guernsey: Guernsey Press Co Ltd, 1988, p 14
52. Letty Russell, *Church in the Round*, Louisville: Westminster/John Knox Press, 1993, p 22

Promising Perspectives

The Second Vatican Council was instrumental in effecting a new but as yet unrealised hope for women in the church. Despite the difficult situation with patriarchy and the non-ordination of women, it is possible to recognise serious efforts on the part of the institutional authorities as authentic. Among the pages of the Council's document *Gaudium et spes* we find, for example, the following: 'At present women are involved in nearly all spheres of life; they ought to be permitted to play their part fully according to their own particular nature. It is up to everyone to see to it that women's specific and necessary participation in cultural life be acknowledged and fostered.'[53] We do well to agree with Anne Patrick when she refers to *Gaudium et spes* as a ground-breaking document. She declares that it struck forcefully on a female population waiting to implement their ideas and take them beyond anything envisaged by the fathers of the council. That document, therefore, paved the way for Christian feminists to find a more adequate vision of justice. This would be particularly true among Catholics who might have been otherwise forced to choose between Catholicism, some other faith tradition, or secular feminism.[54]

Similar ideas about the role of women are also reflected in the three popes of the Second Vatican Council era. Shortly before his death in 1963, Pope John XXIII treats of the rights and obligations affecting persons and societies in the economic and political spheres of life in *Pacem in terris*.[55] He observed that something had occurred in the consciousness of contemporary human experience where women were awakening to free and responsible participation in determining their own lives. He writes: 'Women are gaining an increasing awareness of their natural dignity. Far from being content with a purely passive role, or allowing themselves to be exploited, they are demanding both in domestic and in public life the rights and

---

53. Vatican Council II, *Gaudium et spes*, par 60
54. Anne Patrick, 'Toward Renewing the Life and Culture of Fallen Man: *Gaudium et spes* as Catalyst for Catholic Feminist Theology' in J. Dwyer (ed), *Questions of Special Urgency*, Washington DC: Georgetown University Press, 1986, pp 55-57
55. John XXIII, *Pacem in terris*, London: Catholic Truth Society, 1963

duties which belong to them as human persons.'[56] Paul VI was also becoming ever more conscious of women's place in society and in the church. In his Apostolic Letter, *Octogesima adveniens*, he noted with approval that, 'in many countries a charter for women ... would put an end to actual discrimination and would establish relationships of equality in rights and of respect of their dignity ...'[57] In reference to matters of justice, he teaches that, 'no new phenomenon must be placed on those who are discriminated against in law or in fact, on account of their race, origin, colour, culture, sex or religion'.[58]

John Paul II, in a rather lengthy document of over one hundred pages, wrote his much quoted Apostolic Letter *Mulieris dignitatem* (MD).[59] Despite its reiteration of the non-ordination of women, it contains some very positive statements with respect to the church and women. This pope refers to the anthropomorphism of biblical language and its limitations in referring to God as male (MD 8); he points to the fact that Jesus spent much time talking to women in an age when this was frowned upon (MD 12); he notes the significance of the importance of women as the first witnesses of the resurrection (MD 16) and he views freely chosen virginity as a way in which women can exercise autonomy over their own lives (MD 17). The letter contains many other such positive statements, including the relationship between men and women as a matter of equality, difference and partnership. Even a brief reading of the letter will show that he treats of men and women as equal but different. He debates the point that masculinity and femininity each have distinct characteristics given to them by the Creator. In order to clarify that distinction, he focuses on their respective roles and the part played by women in particular.

Conclusion

It has been shown that indisputable attempts have been made to

---

56. John XXIII, *Pacem in terris*, par 41

57. Paul VI, *Octogesima adveniens* in M. Walsh and B. Davies (eds), *Proclaiming Justice and Peace*, London: Collins Liturgical Publications, 1984, par 13

58. Paul VI, *Octogesima adveniens*, par 16

59. John Paul II, *Mulieris dignitatem*, London: Catholic Truth Society, 1988

take seriously the full humanity and value of the role of women in the official church documents of the Second Vatican Council, the writings of popes John XXIII, Paul VI and John Paul II. These documents are without doubt helpful, sincere and genuine, promising hope for a more progressive attitude towards the equality of women in the church. They also provide great symbolic significance with no hint of women being representative of the sinful Eve which was prominent in certain Christian literature through the ages. Christian feminists, then, should employ everything within the tradition they can to enhance the church community and its work in the world. Alternatively, anything that is patriarchal or restrictive should be challenged with effort and determination, for to walk away from Christ, his message and his church is an unworthy alternative for the true Christian. It is necessary to recognise, however, that although the church's great drawbridge has been lowered in favour of women's advancement, the portcullis is not yet open. What is required is a theology with the ability to do so. It was indicated at the beginning of this chapter that the ecclesiatypical approach, which images Mary as a Type for the church, is one possibility. Through Mary we learn about the ideals of Christian living, specifically within the context of the church as the People of God.

When we turned to the presentation of Mary as a Type for the church we were not prepared to deny her experience as a human being. Like us, she shared the trials and tribulations of life as anyone following Christ must do – she did not just select the 'good bits' of living out the gospel values nor can those who espouse Christian feminism do the same. Certainly Christian feminists must seriously question the weaknesses that lie within the institutional church. They must continue to recount their experiences of the institution, particularly where its patriarchal interpretation of certain aspects of the scriptures and tradition in its treatment of women is found wanting. As if awaking from a time-warp in the second half of the twentieth-century, the rise of feminisms in general, and Christian feminism in particular, unearthed a plethora of women's histories, legends, myths and cultures too potent to quell. In that primordial flush of rediscovery, the theology surrounding Mary was not forsaken.

Through the goodwill and learning of that Christian feminist sensibility, and in accordance with the promise of openness on the part of the church, the following chapter outlines the essence of a *via media* where Mary at the centre of humankind will act as a bridge between the two. Further development of Mary as Ecclesiatype will now be presented as the one who will meet that end, for above all she is the people's Mary.

CHAPTER FIVE

I am Mary

A Via Media

Although Christian feminism is a form of modern philosophical anthropology which often critiques patriarchy and the nature of hierarchical institutions, its proponents do not always pursue paths of extreme radicalism. Theologians who do so are likely to find Marian doctrine irrelevant where Mary, either as a historical or symbolic figure, will be dismissed as extraneous and/or missing from their pages. These latter are not the theologians we are interested in. Writing about Mary with reference to Christian feminist theology, however, is not to suggest that she is the sole possession either of women or indeed is she owned by the institutional church and its doctrines about her. Rather her role is above all about the *ecclesia*, the entire People of God, men and women alike. In the latter respect, we have already shown in chapter three that there is a tradition of imaging Mary as ecclesiatype from the fathers of the church, certain early theologians of both major and minor influence, through the Second Vatican Council and culminating in the works of Paul VI and John Paul II.

In this chapter, we will proceed initially by taking account of two authors who have earned themselves the reputation of Christian feminist theologians, Elizabeth Johnson and Rosemary Ruether. Although neither has written exclusively nor extensively about Mary, they are well-known contemporary scholars who situate her concretely among the People of God. We search in their theology for a *via media* between Catholic Church teaching and Christian feminist hermeneutics which rests comfortably with those who recognise the nature of Mary as fundamental to the life of the church. It is being suggested, therefore, that imaging Mary as ecclesiatype provides one such possible theological medium. However, the term requires further development. In order to develop an understanding of the ecclesiatypical approach as it is being developed here, liberty will be taken with the term 'ecclesiatypical' – employed relatively contiguous to the Second Vatican Council – to emphasise the ecclesiological aspects of Mary's role in the church. Greater account will then be taken of Mary's place in the scriptures, her faith, and her significance as *Mater Ecclesiae,* her discipleship and the meaning of her *Magnificat.* All of these pertain to elements which constitute the essence of the ecclesiatypical approach. More importantly, none of these elements are mutually exclusive either to ecclesiological church teaching or to Christian feminist theology.

Johnson: 'Truly Our Sister'

At the heart of Johnson's Marian theology is a picture of the world inhabited by Mary which takes account of the political, economic, religious and cultural impingements she experienced during her lifetime. The title of Johnson's mariological work *Truly Our Sister*[1] was influenced by Paul VI's *Marialis cultus* where he says: 'Mary in fact is one of our race, a true daughter of Eve … and truly our sister, who as a poor and humble woman fully shared our lot'.[2] Johnson aims to work out a feminist liberation theology of Mary, and there 'to remember her, dangerously and consolingly, as a woman with her own particular history among her contemporaries and before God'.[3] As all theologians who muse about Mary's role in the tradition will admit, Johnson has had to reflect and re-reflect on her own particular theological endeavours, eventually coming to the conclusion that Mary should be situated within the communion of saints. Effectively this means that somewhat greater attention is focused on Mary's concrete historical image, possibly over and above her symbolic one,[4] where her own destiny, ultimately

1. Elizabeth Johnson, *Truly Our Sister,* New York: Continuum, 2003
2. Paul VI, *Marialis cultus,* par 56
3. Johnson, *Truly Our Sister,* p 95
4. See Wolfhart Pannenberg, 'Mary, Redemption, and Unity', *Una Sancta,* Vol 24, No 1 (1967), pp 62-68; See also Raymond Brown, 'The Meaning of Modern New Testament Studies for an Ecumenical Understanding of Mary' in R. Brown (ed), *Biblical Reflections on Crisis Facing the Church,* New York: Paulist Press, p 105. Pannenberg argues that there is a significant for-

like that of all human beings, is oriented towards God.[5]

This is the Mary of the church, Mary as ecclesiatype who is in solidarity with multitudes of women and men in the relentless march of time throughout the centuries. Her life's journey strikes a chord with us today of the displacement of so many misfortunate and tragic people who are separated from their homes and families because of war, violence, poverty, unjust taxation and unscrupulous world leaders. The flight into Egypt (Mt 2:13-14) can be paralleled with countless numbers of refugees fleeing from horrific conditions and fear of death in their attempt to escape to countries that either cannot or will not shelter them. Not even for them, however, is a stable or a manger available. Mary losing her son is reminiscent of the 'Mothers of the Disappeared' in many parts of Latin America. She then becomes sister to women and men who suffer in oppressive and dire circumstances. Johnson believes that we should rediscover Mary for our own generation in order to interpret what she means for today's Christians. This can best be done by studying her in her socio-historical environment which reveals for us her true humanity while at the same time setting her in the context of our own lives. Johnson discloses a viewpoint inclusive of the Holy Spirit and the communion of saints, when she interprets Mary as:

> ... a graced, concrete historical person amid the company of the saints in heaven and on earth ... capable of promoting action on behalf of global justice and liberation, particularly empowering to the flourishing of women, coherent with elements of biblical, classical, and conciliar teaching, and productive of religious sense for our time.[6]

mal difference between christology and mariology. He prefers to image Mary in symbolic terms since, he claims, it does not possess the same historical basis as christology, which is justified through the life, death and resurrection of Jesus the Christ. Brown concurs with Pannenberg, claiming that it was the paucity of scriptural accounts about Mary which permitted her symbolism to explode through the centuries.

5. Johnson, *Truly Our Sister*, pp 95-101
6. Johnson, *Truly Our Sister*, p 113

Johnson is quite at ease with Mary as a historical person.[7] Here she expresses that traditional paradigm as an egalitarian model of common companionship and friendship between humankind and the saints. Based on this encompassing premise she poses the question, 'What would be a theologically sound, ecumenically fruitful, spiritually empowering, ethically challenging, and socially liberating interpretation of Mary for the twenty-first century'?[8] Her rhetorical response is delivered from two perspectives, specifically towards the latter part of her theological deliberations in her main Marian work, *Truly Our Sister*. Firstly, she advises of Mary's historical memory with heavy reference to the scriptures[9] and secondly she visualises her as 'Friend of God and Prophet' – within the communion of saints.[10]

In order to comprehend that socio-historical world of Mary, Johnson returns to the woman behind the biblical texts, to confront the social and cultural settings of the earthly existence of the Mother of God Incarnate. Mary's historical background is illustrated by Johnson's locating her in a particular place and time, even to the point of describing what may have been Mary's actual physical appearance. The oft-told story is worth re-telling if only as a reminder that Mary was of flesh and bone. She was born in the Reign of Herod between 37 BC and AD 4. She was Jewish in appearance, with dark hair and eyes and would have been likely to possess the muscular stature of the Mediterranean peasant women of her day.[11] She worked to feed and clothe her children and she was married to a local carpenter, and both struggled to pay taxes to the Temple, Herod and Rome.[12] She

7. See Elizabeth Johnson, *Friends of God and Prophets: A Feminist Theological Reading of the Communion of Saints*, New York: Continuum, 1998. While exploring the symbols of the Communion of Saints as a context for her Marian theology, Johnson turned to that creedal symbol itself as a historical and doctrinal theme.

8. Johnson, *Truly Our Sister*, p 3

9. Johnson, *Truly Our Sister*, pp 217-297

10. Johnson, *Truly Our Sister*, pp 305-319

11. Johnson, *Truly Our Sister*, p 206

12. See Elizabeth Johnson, 'Jesus the Wisdom of God: A Biblical Basis for Non-Androcentric Christology', *Ephemerides Thologicae Lovanienses*, Vol 61, No 4 (1985), pp 261-294. Johnson is of the opinion, however, that women

worshipped the God of Abraham and Sarah and observed the practices of their Jewish faith by attending the festivals of their religious customs and going to the synagogue.[13]

Although Johnson describes Mary in this way, she is probably not particularly interested in the minutia of her physical characteristics. Rather her intention is to liberate Mary from the accretions of former extravagant symbolism in the belief that she will be revealed as a 'Friend of God and Prophet' within the communion of saints for the *ecclesia* of today. She crafts her own liberating theology of Mary by describing the Mother of God's humble circumstances, 'not as mere historical background but as the warp and woof of the world in which the revelation of God took place'.[14] In this way, Johnson's theology has, for many men and women in Catholic Christianity, carved out a more realistic earth-centred mariology by returning Mary to her roots and reinterpreting an alternative understanding of her through various themes and symbols. In that particular sense, it may be said that Johnson works from an image of Mary as ecclesiatype since it points to Mary as one of the pilgrim People of God on earth. In that context, Johnson's primary image of Mary is one of sisterhood to humankind and friend of God.

Ruether: The Historical Mary

Like Johnson, Ruether, looking at Mary through the eyes of Christian feminism, also takes a keen interest in the historical Mary emphasising that all we really know about her is to be found exclusively in the New Testament. Ruether's Mary is an earthy, realistic one who had to struggle with an apparently recalcitrant Son from the time he got lost in the Temple (Lk 2: 41-49) until his life was brought to a brutal end on a Roman cross (Lk 23:26-49). It is well known that the accounts of the historical Mary are sparse and a glance at the New Testament will reveal

---

were not always insignificant at this time due to competing female deities such as the Egyptian goddess Isis. The characteristics of Isis were to be found in Yahweh's *Hokmah* who was imaged as female. *Hokmah* affirmed God's presence in feminine terms. This elevated the status of women to some extent.

13. Johnson, *Truly Our Sister*, pp 162-166
14. Johnson, *Truly Our Sister*, p 206

only a paucity of references to her. Ruether reiterates this point in stating that there is little allusion to Mary either historically or symbolically in the New Testament.

In Paul's Letter to the Galatians (Gal 4:4), he does not even mention Mary by name but simply refers to her as a woman who brought forth a Son under the law. Only the gospels and Acts provide Mary with her name.[15] In Matthew, it is Joseph who holds the leading role and plays the decisive part, while Mary appears relegated to the status of passivity. Again, it is Joseph who receives the two vital messages from the angel predicting the miracle birth and the directive to flee from his home to Egypt in order to secure the safety of the mother and baby. When Joseph found out about the pregnancy, his intention was to divorce Mary but he decided against it upon hearing the voice of the angel. Joseph's significance in Matthew, therefore, appears to be stronger than that of Mary, borne out also in his delineation of Jesus' genealogy which he traces to Joseph through the Davidic line.[16]

The above familiar account of Matthew's narrative is used by Ruether to show that he does not make of Mary a particularly important figure. Her lowliness in Matthew portrays a patriarchal telling of the story, passively situating her as a plebeian in the drama of salvation. Mary's relatively insignificant status as a humble woman becomes clearer when we remember that her pregnancy actually greatly disturbed Joseph. He had legal rights over her. If he found that she was pregnant by another man, Joseph could have had her put to death according to the strict letter of the law. The would-be foster father is thus left with a dilemma. Although he wishes to show kindness to Mary, Joseph must also satisfy the requirement of the legal system of that day and culture. In order to solve his problem, he decides to serve Mary privately with a document of divorce. Apparently at that particular time he does not ask himself how this would protect Mary from public shame if the child were to be born out of wedlock.[17]

---

15. Elizabeth Johnson, 'The Symbolic Character of Theological Statements about Mary', *Journal of Ecumenical Studies*, Vol 22, (1985), p 316. See also Hans Küng, *On Being a Christian*, London: Collins, 1974.

16. Ruether, *Mary – The Feminine Face of the Church*, p 32

17. See John Meier, *Matthew*, Dublin: Veritas, 1980, pp 6-7

Ruether separates the Matthean and Lukan stories to elucidate the latter evangelist's different perspective, pointing to the fact that they are often fused in our minds when we hear them.[18] For Luke, Mary is the key figure where she takes centre stage in his infancy narrative gospel. The angel, not Joseph, visits her in her human and historical circumstance, speaks to her and determines a positive response from her. Mary then travels to visit her cousin Elizabeth (Lk 1:39-45) with Luke offering no indication that she had informed her future spouse about the journey or about her conception. Where Matthew states simply that Jesus is born, Luke puts Mary at the centre of the birth (Lk 2:2-7). Mary is also active in another sense. She wonders about her son and the mystery of it all as she, 'remembered all these things and thought deeply about them' (Lk 2:19). In the same way, Luke has Simeon address Mary specifically with the prediction: 'And sorrow, like a sharp sword, will break your own heart' (Lk 2:34). Again when the young Jesus at twelve years of age displays his knowledge in the Temple, it is Mary who takes the initiative to admonish him with the words: 'My son, why have you done this to us? Your father and I have been terribly worried trying to find you (Lk 2:48).[19]

Of the two well known accounts above, Matthew's Mary, the historical mother of Jesus is a passive woman waiting to be told how to react to an extraordinary situation. In Luke, she is a woman of independence co-operating with God through the angelic messenger without help either from her spouse or anyone else. Nonetheless, in neither of these situations does Mary come across as anything other than a human mother and woman of the world, anxious for the welfare of her child and to do the will of God. There is nothing in church teaching that would not be in accord with either Johnson or Ruether in these accounts of the historical Mary (albeit that the latter theologian tends at times towards a rather simplistic fundamental interpretation). Ruether obviously prefers the Lukan version of events, which is also the choice of the Second Vatican Council fathers in relating the incarnation story.[20] Each in their own way

---

18. Ruether, *Mary – The Feminine Face of the Church*, pp 33-34
19. Ruether, *Mary – The Feminine Face of the Church*, pp 33-34
20. Vatican Council II, *Lumen gentium*, pars 56, 57, 58, 66

depends on the scriptures to ground their Marian theology. Indeed, one of the greatest successes of the Second Vatican Council was its return to the scriptures for evidence of Mary's role in the history of salvation. For the council, Mary is the one who freely gave her consent to conceive the Son of God. *Lumen gentium* advises that this consent was not something passive in Mary's life; rather it required her free co-operation through her faith and obedience.[21] The two popes writing subsequent to the council, Paul VI and John Paul II, as we have already seen in chapter three above, are also of the same mind.[22]

Both Ruether's and Johnson's Marian perspectives, and these three sources from the *magisterium*, show that there is common agreement to be found among them in their understanding of Mary's historical function in the mystery of salvation. From an ecclesiatypical viewpoint they all ground the historical Mary within the confines of her culture, showing the limitations placed on her and revealing in particular those limitations for women at the time. Here is the backdrop to recognising a woman who would have found it very difficult to rise above the station in society wherein she was situated. Mary's humanness and struggle within this context is at the core of the ecclesiatypical approach. That struggle implies a constant faith and one which must have, at times, put Mary sorely to the test.

The Faith of Mary

Despite the sparsity of scriptural references to Mary, they nonetheless portray her very human profile and in this respect we appreciate that she identifies historically with the People of God, specifically in the robustness of her faith. She cannot comprehend her Son's mission yet loyally she remains with him from womb to tomb. If we choose to accept at face value Ruether's literal interpretation of Luke's gospel, form and redaction criticism not withstanding, it would appear that Mary did not receive much gratitude from her Son in return for her loyalty. Some of the most significant passages suggest Jesus' rejection of his family in favour of his mission. For example, he

21. Vatican Council II, *Lumen gentium*, pars 55, 56, 57
22. Paul VI, *Marialis cultus*, pars 8, 9; John Paul 11, *Mary Mother of the Redeemer*, pars 12, 13, 14, 15, 16

taught that those who would be saved must be ready to leave their families to follow him (Lk 12:49-53); he disputed that he was his mother's son, preferring to pursue his mission (Lk 11:27-28) and subsequent to his resurrection he chose to appear to Mary Magdalene and other female disciples but not to his mother (Lk 24:1-12).[23]

It is well known that the fourth gospel is replete with sophist-icated theological symbolism. However, a *verbatim* approach to its account of the Cana marriage wine shortage permits us to imagine ourselves at the side of the human Mary. When the wine runs out she approaches her son. In response to her request to do something about the deficient wine jars, he replies rather abruptly, it would appear: 'You must not tell me what to do' (Jn 2:4). Yes, there are scholarly exegetical interpretations of this passage[24] such is the wealth of all the gospel stories. However, if we accept that retort as we read it, it seems a disrespectful one since it would not be expected that a decently reared young man would speak to his own mother in this way. The wise Mary, nonetheless, simply ignores him and directs the servants to 'Do whatever he tells you' (Jn 2:5). These encounters speak of a woman working through an extraordinary set of circumstances but she does so based entirely on her faith, paying no heed to her own lack of understanding of her son's mission. Standing at the side of Mary, it would not be difficult to see how this relationship must have at times been emotionally, psycholog-ically and spiritually bewildering for the mother.

Let us not forget however, that despite Mary's lack of comprehension of the great mystery into which she is drawn she said 'Yes' (Lk 1:38) at the annunciation. That momentary response of a young girl taken completely by surprise was probably the most exacting contract ever to have been requested by God of a human being. Yet, 'Yes' she exclaimed and she continued to live out that promise in faith and trust, regardless of her son's apparent lack of concern for his own life. Or, as Susan McCaslin writes poetically of it: 'She [Mary] must have seen the blunt nose

23. Ruether, *Mary – The Feminine Face of the Church*, pp 37-38

24. Bruce Vawter, 'The Gospel According to John' in R. Brown, J. Fitzmyer and R. Murphy (eds), *The Jerome Biblical Commentary*, London: Geoffrey Chapman, 1981, pp 427-428

of death when he set his face steadily toward Jerusalem and perhaps it was right and perhaps there was no other way.'[25] Somehow deep down inside Mary's faith she knew there could be no other way and her 'Yes' bears unquestionable witness to this.

Hans Von Balthasar runs part of the gamut of Mary's life with Jesus in his particular rendering of her faithful 'Yes' in the following summary:

> What is basic to the infinite elasticity of the Marian Yes is that it again and again stretches beyond understanding and must consent to what is not within the domain of the humanly possible, foreseeable, bearable or fitting. It must embrace virginal conception by an already married woman, her 'not understanding' the reply of her twelve-year-old, to her being painfully rebuffed by her son (some twenty years later) and finally her being abandoned at the foot of the Cross and committed to 'another son', John ... These events repeatedly challenge her understanding and demand an endlessly growing readiness (without any resistance).[26]

In this way of thinking, Balthasar tells of a woman who gradually understands that her offspring is the suffering Messiah, albeit taking the effort of a lifetime for her to do so. To recap so far, both Balthasar and Ruether embrace Mary as a woman of faith, but it is the faith of a mother often confused and hurt by the apparent aloofness and abrasiveness of her own child. Yet, such is the strength of her faith that she never abandons him. Nowhere in the gospels does Mary appear out of the presence of her son. From the annunciation to the cross, she

---

25. Susan McCaslin, 'Mary Mother', *Journal of Feminist Studies in Religion*, Vol 23, No 1 (2007), p 51

26. Hans Von Balthasar, *The Office of Peter and the Structure of the Church*, San Francisco: Ignatius Press, 1986. See also Peter Bearsley, 'Mary the Perfect Disciple: A Paradigm for Mariology', *Theological Studies*, Vol 43, No 3 (1980), p 486. Bearsley, however, would disagree with this viewpoint. He says of the Cana story, for example, that Mary does not feel rebuffed by Jesus' reply and that there has not been a rupture in their relationship. Bearsley's reasoning is that if Mary had felt her requests rejected in some way she would not have gone to the waiter to tell them to do whatever her son had commanded.

is at his side despite his continual surprising of her and her pondering bewilderment. Mary's faith never gives up but continues to grow in strength and understanding. It is a faith close to the struggle that takes place in the human heart of every believer and one with which the person of faith is well able to identify.

We encounter the challenge to Mary's faith and its growth also in John Paul II. His identification with her anxiety about her mysterious son is palpable in certain aspects of his phraseology. For example, he quotes Vatican II as he sees Mary at the annunciation embarking on a 'pilgrimage of faith'; he compares her faith to that of Abraham's for just like him she had to, 'hope against hope'; through all these 'trials and adversities', Mary holds fast to her faith throughout her life with Jesus which she does with a 'heaviness of heart'; she experiences, as all people of faith must, a 'kind of veil through which one has to draw near to the Invisible One and to live in intimacy with the mystery'. This pope reiterates at length that to be faithful, using Mary as a model, considerable effort must be taken on the part of the believer. Furthermore, John Paul II adds, 'to believe means to abandon oneself' to the truth of the word of the living God, knowing and humbly recognising 'how unsearchable are his judgements and how inscrutable his ways' (Rom 11:33)'. So be it that Mary was willing to pay the price and walk through her life with nothing more to accompany her on this earth than the 'dim light of faith'.[27] Whether one is a Christian feminist or a Pontiff, the Mary of real life, the Mary of the scriptures and the Mary of faith are all elements in the ecclesiatypical approach. This approach unites and identifies them as people who ponder the intrigues and mysteries of their faith and pay the price, for better or for worse, as Christianity requires throughout the course of their lifetimes.

Mater Ecclesiae and the Question of Motherhood
Perhaps it is best to mention again at this stage that relevant themes in the ecclesiatypical approach include the historical human context of Mary's life, her faith and her discipleship. All

---

27. John Paul II, *Mary Mother of the Redeemer*, pars 14, 15, 16, 17, 18

of these come from the basis of her relationship with the church which is not at variance in general either with church teaching or Christian feminist theology. In that context and in relation to her motherhood, we now make reference to the title of Mary as *Mater Ecclesiae* (Mother of the Church). The Polish bishops announced that this designation should be officially launched at the Second Vatican Council. Furthermore, the presiding pope at that time, John XXIII, wished for it to be conferred on Mary. However, the Commission which prepared *Lumen gentium* rejected the title. They did so on the grounds that it set Mary above the church, departing from the original patristic theme of *Ecclesia Mater* (the church as mother). Nonetheless, the *Mater Ecclesiae* title holds significant enough meaning for a number of authors to have made reference to it in their writings. Christian feminist theologian Anne Carr's study, for example, reveals that although the title is not contained in *Lumen gentium*, it is implied in several of its passages where the Calvary account in particular, 'vividly suggests [Mary's] maternal relationship to the church'.[28] The passage reads:

> Thus the Blessed Virgin advanced in her pilgrimage of faith, and faithfully persevered in her union with her son unto the cross, where she stood, in keeping with the divine plan, enduring with her only begotten son the intensity of his suffering, associated herself with his sacrifice in her mother's heart, and lovingly consenting to the immolation of this victim which was born of her. Finally, she was given by the same Christ Jesus dying on the cross as a mother to his disciple, with these words: 'Woman, behold thy son' (Jn 19:26-27).[29]

For Carr, the inclusion of this passage in the *Lumen gentium* chapter of the Vatican Council documents is an indication that Mary is to be recognised as a Type of the church within the context of her motherhood.[30] Mary as *Mater Ecclesiae* tells of her part in the tradition as one who walks among the pilgrim People of God. She accompanies them on their journey down through

---

28. Carr, 'Mary in the Mystery of the Church', p 16
29. Vatican Council II, *Lumen gentium*, par 58
30. Carr, 'Mary in the Mystery of the Church', p 17

the centuries as their mother in the context of her humanity and all that this association entails.

Mary's motherhood of itself bespeaks a certain symbolic relationship that members of the church relate to through her earthiness and love of her child. If Mary is Mother of the Church then we must be, by definition, brothers and sisters of Christ. John Paul II puts forward his description of Mary's motherhood in that context through the Cana story when he writes:

> ... the description of the Cana event outlines what is actually manifested as a new kind of motherhood according to the spirit and not just according to the flesh, that is to say Mary's solicitude for human beings, her coming to them in the wide variety of their wants and needs.[31]

He continues: 'Mary "puts herself in the middle", that is to say ... not as an outsider, but in her position as mother.'[32] With this title, then, Mary is depicted as a very human figure since a mother is one who understands the hungry faith of her children as she herself gives heart and soul to their needs. Carr takes this aspect of Mary's empathetic motherhood perhaps too far, however, when she claims that the *Mater Ecclesiae* mother struggled with her faith until the end of her own life and only then did she become a member of the believing community.[33] This latter interpretation can hardly be sustained especially where we find in the Acts of the Apostles that Mary gathered frequently to pray with the apostles and other women of their group (Acts 1:13-14). Nonetheless, we see that Carr, from her own Christian feminist perspective, is endeavouring to emphasise the point that Mary as mother is not to be taken as a model of static perfection but as a dynamic model of human faith and struggle.

John Paul II further develops his particular account of Mary's motherhood when he apportions special prominence to motherhood itself, describing, in his Apostolic Letter *Mulieris dignitatem*, how this along with virginity is one of the most important life experiences for a women. He illustrates thus: 'We

---

31. John Paul II, *Mary Mother of the Redeemer*, par 21
32. John Paul II, *Mary Mother of the Redeemer*, par 21
33. Carr, *Transforming Grace*, pp 194-197

must now focus our meditation on virginity and motherhood as two particular dimensions of the fufilment of the female personality'.[34] A word of caution, however, is exercised by Johnson of an overemphasis on Mary's motherhood alone. She is concerned that this aspect of Mary's role has been so strongly portrayed in the tradition that it presents as the sole reason for her life and her existence. Johnson emphasises prudence when she advises: 'I want to be very careful here, since holding up Mary's motherhood as a model for all women is one of the neuralgic points in traditional mariology ... it becomes clear that not all women want to be mothers, nor need they be in order to be true women.'[35] She is stressing the position that we must avoid too exclusive an emphasis on Mary's motherhood – a concern that is not entirely without warrant.

Although we may presume that the majority of women have experienced being mothered, not all have experienced motherhood. In imaging Mary as *Mater Ecclesiae*, the church community may need to take greater heed of the essence of womanhood exclusive of motherhood, since not for every woman is that always the highest purpose of the meaning of womanhood. Nevertheless, it may be said in favour of John Paul's 'motherhood' passages, that he grounds Mary in her humanness for he recognises that Mary is united intimately with the church. She is also 'present in the midst of the pilgrim church from generation to generation through faith and as the model of the hope which does not disappoint'.[36] Mary walking in the midst of a pilgrim people illustrates again what the ecclesiatypical approach is about. It is an image of Mary as an ordinary woman with an extraordinary story and how she copes with that mystery in the course of a lifetime.

Imaging Mary as *Mater Ecclesiae*, then, stems from an understanding of her special ability to identify with humankind as a mother figure, particularly with those who suffer socially, politically and spiritually in the world. Few can dispute that this image has flourished among the poorest of the poor,

---

34. John Paul II, *Mulieris dignitatem*, par 17
35. Johnson, *Truly Our Sister*, p 286
36. John Paul II, *Mother of the Redeemer*, par 42

particularly those struggling to survive in so many different ways in the majority world. Mary's image as Mother of the Church provides an identity and potent image for all oppressed peoples. The peoples of Latin America, for example, have been exemplary in their fidelity to Mary, empathising with her lack of social standing during her allotted time on this earth. One might well agree with Els Maeckelberghe when she says that the 'Mary of the liberation theologies is a challenge to Western theologies'.[37] Mary, like them, needed Christ's redemption but, more importantly, they acknowledge that she has completed her journey and kept her faith. Central to that particular genre of theology is the *Magnificat* which tells of God's 'preferential option for the poor'.[38]

Mary's Magnificat

A recurrent element in the ecclesiatypical approach, then, is about appreciation of Mary as one the People of God and a living member of that community on earth. In every sense Mary suffers and struggles with those to whom she is akin. Nowhere is Mary as ecclesiatype more clearly reflected than in the *Magnificat*. This woman of symbolic liberation has a special, heartfelt message which she proclaims in that great Marian prayer text of the gospel of Luke (1:46-55). The *Magnificat* is echoed in the hymn of Hannah, the mother of Samuel, one thousand years before Mary:

> The Lord kills and restores to life; he sends people to the world of the dead and brings them back again. He makes some men poor and others rich; he humbles some and makes others great. He lifts the poor from the dust and raises the needy from their misery. He makes them companions of princes and puts them in places of honour (1 Sam 2:6-8).

In this ancient passage, we see Hannah, Samuel's mother, who is in favour with God, a once barren woman now gifted with a son, liberated and thus relieved of her shame. Equally the

---

37. Els Maeckelberghe, *Desperately Seeking Mary*, Kampen: Kok Pharos, 1991, p 11
38. Dermot Lane, *Foundations for a Social Theology*, Dublin: Gill and Macmillan, 1984, pp 21-22; 120

Magnificat may be interpreted as a true song of liberation, one which sits comfortably with Mary as ecclesiatype and common both to Christian feminism and church teaching. In the *Magnificat*, we encounter the fruit of that dialogue between Mary and God. It is a prayer of praise coming forth from the heart proclaiming the greatness, the goodness and the mercy of God:

> He has stretched out his mighty arm and scattered the proud with all their plans. He has brought down mighty kings from their thrones and lifted up the lowly. He has filled the hungry with good things and sent the rich away with empty hands. He has kept the promise he made to our ancestors and has come to the help of his servant Israel (Lk 1:51-54).

Mary is closely allied to God's preferential option for the poor and the part played by the church. When God enters history through Christ, a liberating revolution takes place in human relationships. Ruether reminds us that through Mary this revolution is put into effect where she herself is the one who embodies and personifies oppressed and subjected peoples of all time.[39] Likewise Paul VI represents Mary not only as the sturdy advocate of the oppressed but, conscious of women in the church, he portrays her as a woman of action and resolve. He also clarifies that relationship between Mary and the church when he says that the Spirit came down on the infant church in the Upper Room where the Mother of Jesus and the apostles were present.[40] This pope further notes that Mary should not be thought only of as 'a mother exclusively concerned with her own divine son, but rather as a woman whose action helped to strengthen the apostolic community's faith in Christ'.[41]

In *Redemptoris mater*, John Paul II is also so taken with the significance of the *Magnificat* that he quotes the prayer in full.[42] When the church makes that all-important preferential option for the poor it becomes intimately involved with the Christian

---

39. Ruether, *Sexism and God-Talk*, p 155
40. Paul VI, *Marialis cultus*, par 26
41. Paul VI, *Marialis cultus*, par 37
42. John Paul II, *Mary Mother of the Redeemer*, par 35

understanding of liberation.[43] Ruether reiterates John Paul's interpretation of the *Magnificat* in a speech which he made at the Conference of Latin American bishops (CELAM, 1979).[44] Of his liberation Marian theology she says that it is, 'perhaps one of the most important new theological themes to emerge in the pope's speeches ... the bishops follow the pope in echoing this theme at various points of the final document'.[45] It is clear for Ruether that the pope images Mary as the personification of the New Israel, the church, especially when it is representative of the marginalised of this earth. Of special interest to Ruether is the fact that the document recognises the inclusion of women among those who are oppressed. Through Mary, women in some special way, personify the oppressed.[46] Of certain import is the fact that it is a woman, Mary, who bridges our understanding of church and what it means to be a follower of Christ. It is indeed within this milieu of discipleship that Mary of Nazareth assumes a most significant place as ecclesiatype.

Mary as Disciple

Mary's discipleship establishes her as one of Jesus' followers on earth. This is compatible with the ecclesiatypical approach for it is an important dimension of her creature-hood and one to which all followers of Christ have the capacity to relate. Like millions of other human beings, Mary followed this man through her dark nights of sorrow and despair. She was true to his call in a way that some of his other followers were not, for we know that there were those who abandoned him while he was about to be led to the cross (Mt 26:55; 69-74). As a disciple, she believed but was not immediately rewarded, unlike Mary Magdalene, for example, who was one of the first to receive an appearance from Jesus after his death (Mk 16:9). Although there is no evidence (at least not according to Western Christian tradition) that Mary of Nazareth received a resurrection

---

43. John Paul II, *Mary Mother of the Redeemer*, par 37
44. Rosemary Ruether, 'Consciousness Raising at Puebla', *Christianity and Crisis*, Vol No 39 (1979), pp 77-79
45. Ruether, *Puebla*, p 80
46. Ruether, *Puebla*, p 79

appearance, unlike the doubting Thomas (Jn 20:24-29) she remained steadfast in her faith. In the same way today, the faithful followers of Christ identify with Mary, her call and her experience of discipleship because, like her, he has not yet appeared to them in physical form.

This true disciple was a woman with a strong sense of her own identity and personhood. She, as a disciple of Jesus, had the courage to make choices, and mistakes possibly, in trying to encourage him to limit his preaching even when it was clear from the scriptures that he might send her away. For example, he was talking to people when his mother and brothers arrived to see him but when he was told that they were outside the house he responded, 'Who is my mother? Who are my brothers?' Then as he looked at the people around him he said, 'Look! Here are my mother and my brothers! Whoever does what God wants him to do, is my brother, my sister, my mother' (Mk 3:31-33). Although Jesus was teaching about discipleship, it may have come across as a rebuff to his mother. However, despite the many times Mary must have been bewildered by what was asked of her by God, she was a true disciple of her son. At the end of it all, Mary did not turn away because the scripture places her after the death of Jesus with the other disciples in the Upper Room (Acts 1:12).

Women may also identify with this earthly understanding of Mary as Disciple. Although discipleship is the necessary means of following Christ for all Christians, John Paul II adverts in particular to the part played by women in the scriptures:

> From the beginning of Christ's mission, women show to him and to his mystery a special sensitivity which is characteristic of their femininity. It must also be said that this is especially confirmed in the paschal mystery, not only at the cross but also at the dawn of the resurrection. The women are the first at the tomb. They are the first to find it empty. They are the first to hear: 'He is not here. He has risen, as he said' (Mt 28:6). They are the first to embrace his feet (cf Mt 28:9). They are also the first to be called to announce this truth to the apostles (cf Mt 28:1-10; Lk 24:8-11).[47]

47. John Paul II, *Mulieris dignitatem*, par 16

A Christian feminist interpretation of discipleship inclusive of Mary is not at odds with this teaching, according to Ruether's reading particularly of Luke's gospel. She points out that among his stories of social iconoclasm, a large number account for the exoneration of women. These include poor women, despised women, widows, the unclean, prostitutes and Samaritans. Those are they in whom the messianic prophet finds the faith that is absent among the so-called righteous of Israel. Other specific examples such as the story of the widow's mite, the forgiveness of the prostitute who has faith, the healing of the woman with a flow of blood and the defence of Mary's right to discipleship are among the Lucan stories which lift up the typology of women as people of faith.[48]

Conclusion

Throughout this chapter, a way of imaging Mary has been proposed that is not inconsistent with official Catholic Church teaching but would also serve as a mediatory theology acceptable to its Christian feminists. We focused primarily, though not exclusively, on two authors, Elizabeth Johnson and Rosemary Ruether, who have remained within the church throughout their lives. Despite their loyal criticism of it on certain issues, these specifically relate to the church's unequal regard for women in its tradition which was treated of to some extent in chapter four above. Although neither theologian has focused her scholarly works exclusively on Mary, they presented enough Marian material to claim a theology common both to church teaching and to Christian feminism. In this respect, the ecclesiatypical approach to Marian theology was deemed a satisfactory *via media* especially, as it was shown in chapter three, how it sat comfortably in the writings of the early fathers, the Second Vatican Council, Paul VI and John Paul II.

The ecclesiatypical approach consists of certain elements that take specific account of Mary's historicity, her place in the scriptures, her faith, her significance as *Mater Ecclesiae*, her discipleship and the meaning of her *Magnificat*. What is particularly noteworthy about this approach is that it casts Mary

---

48. Ruether, *Sexism and God-Talk*, p 156

in the light of normal womanhood liberating her for all women and men. Within that context, women in particular have symbolic priority with Mary as one who is a model of encouragement and liberation. Mary now becomes a dynamic model of earthly, human struggle, the model of a pilgrim people in solidarity with Jesus and each other in their journey towards God. Her biological motherhood has been revitalised and her faith in the Word of God has been highlighted. If women were asked to identify with an image of Mary as most representative of their sex, perhaps they would choose one which relieves her of being the ideal feminine and permits her simply to be herself – that is Mary as ecclesiatype.

This chapter will conclude with just one example of Mary as ecclesiatype captured in essence through the nostalgic, living memory of our own Irish poet, Seamus Heaney (b. 1939):

My sensibility was formed by the dolorous murmurings of the rosary, and the generally Marian quality of devotion. The reality that was addressed was maternal, and the posture was one of supplication ... The attitude to life that was inculcated into me – not by priests, but by the active, lived thing of prayers and so on, in my house through my mother – was really patience ... In practice, the shrines, the rosary beads, all the devotions, were centred towards a feminine presence, which I think was terrific for the sensibility. I think that the 'Hail Mary' is more of a poem than the 'Our Father'. 'Our Father' is between chaps, but there is something faintly amorous about the 'Hail Mary'.[49]

It is possible to see in this short extract, certain elements of the ecclesiatypical approach as it manifests itself through the religious practice of Heaney's childhood household. Faith is the bedrock of that home. Mary, through her historical, personal and very real presence is primarily the spiritual conduit of the family's faith to God in heaven. The 'dolorous murmurings of the rosary' reflect the supplications, the hope and praise of God found in the great *Magnificat* (no doubt real to a man who knew

---

49. Michael Parker, *Seamus Heaney: The Making of the Poet*, Basingstoke: University of Iowa Press, 1993, pp 2-5

too well the ravages of war-torn Northern Ireland where he was born). Mary as *Mater Ecclesiae* is undoubtedly symbolised in his little family community (of nine children) as a microcosm of the greater church community. His belief in Mary's maternal accompaniment through association with his own mother's prayer and patience; his conviction that Mary's 'feminine presence' was an integral part of their general domesticity; the daring statement that, 'there is something faintly amorous about the "Hail Mary"' reveals the family custom of love and constant recourse to Christ through rosary repetition. Finally, we sense in the entire excerpt, Mary living as a disciple in their own home, sharing their bread, their prayers, their trials and tribulations, all the while watching over them like she did her own son through the crosses of this life and beyond.

Conclusion

The combining of two ideas was the rationale behind the writing of this book. The first objective was to take a fresh account of ways in which Mary the Mother of God has been understood in Catholic Christianity throughout the centuries. In order to do so, a new set of three Marian types was introduced which would encapsulate just some of the more important time-honoured doctrines, titles, themes, portrayals and images of the great Marian mystery. These three types were termed the theatypical, the christatypical and the ecclesiatypical approaches, each representing Mary as theatype, Mary as christatype and Mary as ecclesiatype respectively. In terms of understanding Mary as she has been imaged and honoured in the tradition, it was shown that devotion and honour to her could be encapsulated in the types. The theatypical approach is a way of seeing Mary as having supremacy almost akin to that of God. The christatypical approach places Mary in such close proximity to Christ that she has the ability to co-redeem, co-mediate and to act as intercessor between humankind and God notwithstanding the unique mediatorship role of Christ her son. The ecclesiatypical approach is as a way of imaging Mary from the perspective of her humanity and how in that capacity she is uniquely present to the church as the People of God. Each of these approaches, not necessarily exclusive of one another, presents an understanding of Mary which is evident from the time of the early fathers through the ages until today

The Marian typologies present a means of categorising, albeit in a very limited way, some of the material that constitutes the great mystery of the Mother of God incarnate. Reflecting upon these types, it is possible to discern how every generation through the ages has tended to make Mary into its own image and likeness. It seems reasonably certain that there really is no singular time-honoured way of appraising Mary, given her multifarious and myriad images. As a symbol and icon of the ages, she has often met the fate of a fragmented existence and has been paraded around for good or ill depending on the vantage or disadvantage point of the author, the devotee, the disenchanted or the distraught. She has been put on a pedestal by some as the 'eternal feminine' but she has also been 'demoted' by others and radically shrunk sometimes to appease a mind-set that denies, is uncomfortable with, or is threatened by, any glorification of the Nazarene village woman with a claim to the title 'Queen of Heaven'.

The second objective in writing this book was to provide a way of addressing difficulties raised by those who recognise the less than satisfactory position of the role of women in the church as it exists and has continued to exist throughout the centuries. The Marian tradition was searched for evidence of a *via media* between Catholic Church teaching and Christian feminist hermeneutics. This was not to prove easy, given that anyone who is interested in the study of Mary of Nazareth is acutely aware of the paradoxes and apparent contradictions in Marian theology. However, the search provided – specifically through the ecclesiatypical approach – a promise of the commonly shared theology which was being sought. Of particular relevance are the key elements contained in the imaging of Mary as ecclesiatype such as her historicity, her place in the scriptures, her faith, her significance as *Mater Ecclesiae* and her discipleship. Add to that her very own special hymn, the *Magnificat*, which she is said to have intoned with joy upon meeting her elderly pregnant cousin Elizabeth (Lk 1:46-55). In this respect, all men and women are able to identify with the human Mary, model of encouragement and liberation, as they tread the very path she trod to the cross and beyond.

Imaging Mary as ecclesiatype, then, may well mean that it is not necessary for Christian feminists, particularly those who are members of the Catholic Church, to stand outside of their faith tradition simply on the basis of the church's patriarchal or hierarchal structure alone. Christian feminists do not pretend that the theologies they propose are fixed or unchanging, nor do they claim to possess the truth. Rather, many are aware that to

be members of that great institution they must remain within it
and patiently encourage dialogue with those who make the
rules. In addition, sincere efforts have been made by the church
authorities to come to terms with the exclusion of women's
experience, specifically at the time of the Second Vatican
Council, in the writings of Paul VI and John Paul II.
Furthermore, it would be unwise to suggest that all men in the
upper echelons of the hierarchy necessarily agree with the
patriarchal structure within which they themselves operate. A
firm conviction remains, therefore, that to abandon the ecclesial
community is not to challenge patriarchy – a systematic
structure that has served neither the plan of Christ nor the
faithful well. The reality of that situation has to be faced with
honesty, dignity and courage by every member of the church.
Ecclesiastical communities are in existence essentially because
they are not supposed to be about their own self-aggrandise-
ment but instead to restore and uphold the Reign of God as it is
found in the Christian message. A final reminder to this effect
comes from an extract in the chapter on Mary in *Lumen gentium*:
'Having entered deeply into the history of salvation, Mary, in a
way, unites in her person and re-echoes the most important
doctrines of the faith: and when she is the subject of preaching
and worship she prompts the faithful to come to her son, to his
sacrifice and to the love of the Father.'[1]

1. Vatican Council II, *Lumen gentium*, par 65

Bibliography

Allen Rabuzzi, K., 'The Socialist Feminist Vision of Rosemary Radford Ruether: A Challenge to Liberal Feminism', *Religious Studies Review*, Vol 15, No 1 (1989), pp 4-8

Ambrose, 'Letters to Bishops' in Deferrari (ed), *The Fathers of the Church*, Washington DC: Catholic University of America Press, 1967, pp 67-205

— 'On the Death of His Brother Satyrus' in Deferrari (ed), *The Fathers of the Church*, Washington DC: Catholic University of America Press, 1968, pp 159-259

— 'The Holy Spirit' in Deferrari (ed), *The Fathers of the Church*, Washington DC: Catholic University of America Press, 1963, pp 35-213

Anglican/Roman Catholic International Commission, J. Yarnold and H. Chadwick (eds), *An ARCIC Catechism*, London: Catholic Truth Society, 1983

Anglican/Roman Catholic Joint Preparatory Commission, 'Authority in the Church 11' [online] http://www.prounione.urbe.it/diaint/arcic/doc/i_arcic_authority2.html [Accessed 31 October 2007].

Balasuriya, T., *Mary and Human Liberation*, London: Mowbray, 1997

Bastero, J. L., *Mary, Mother of the Redeemer*, Dublin: Four Courts Press, 2006

Bates, S., 'The Stained-Glass Ceiling', *The Tablet*, Vol 28, (2004), pp 4-6

Bearsley, P., 'Mary the Perfect Disciple: A Paradigm for Mariology', *Theological Studies*, Vol 43, (1980), pp 461-504

Beattie, T., 'Mary in Patristic Theology' in S. Boss (ed), *Mary the Complete Resource*, New York: OUP, 2007, pp 75-105

Behr-Sigel, E., 'Mary and Women' in M. Plekon *et al* (eds), *Discerning the Sign of the Times: The Vision of Elisabeth Behr-Sigel*, New York: St Vladimir's Seminary Press, 2001

Berry, J., '*Redemptoris Mater* and the Challenge of the Marian Year' *Priests and People*, Vol 1, No 7 (1987), pp 269-274

Bingemer, M., 'Woman: Time and Eternity the Eternal Woman and the Feminine Face of God', *Concilium*, Vol 6, (1991), pp 98-107

Blackbourn, D., *Marpingen Apparitions of the Virgin Mary in Bismarckian Germany*, Oxford: Clarendon Press, 1993

Boff, L., *Church, Charism and Power*, New York: Crossroad, 1981

— *The Maternal Face of God*, London: Collins, 1987

Borresen, K., 'Mary in Catholic Theology', *Concilium*, Vol 168, (1983), pp 48-56

Boss, S., 'The Development of the Doctrine of Mary's Immaculate Conception' in S. Boss (ed), *Mary the Complete Resource*, New York: OUP, 2007, pp 207-235

— 'The Title Theotokos' in S. Boss (ed), *Mary the Complete Resource*, New York: OUP, 2007, pp 50-55

Brown, R. *et al*, *Mary in the New Testament*, New York: Paulist Press, 1978

— 'The meaning of Modern New Testament Studies for an Ecumenical Understanding of Mary' in R. Brown (ed), *Biblical Reflections on Crisis Facing the Church*, New York: Paulist Press, 1975

— 'The Problem of the Virginal Conception of Jesus', *Theological Studies*, Vol 33, (1972), pp 3-34

Bourke, U., *The Bull 'Ineffabilis'*, Dublin: J. Mullaney, 1868.

Cannon, K., 'Erotic Justice: Authority, Resistance, and Transformation' *Journal of Feminist Studies in Religion*, Vol 23, No 1 (2007), pp 22-25

Carr, A., 'Mary in the Mystery of the Church: Vatican Council II' in C. F. Jegen (ed), *Mary According to Women*, Kansas City: Sheed and Ward, 1985, pp 5-32

— *Transforming Grace*, San Francisco: Harper and Row, 1988

Carroll, D., *Towards a Story of the Earth*, Dublin: Dominican Publications, 1987

Christ, C., and Plaskow, J., *Womanspirit Rising: A Feminist Reading in Religion*, San Francisco: Harper and Row, 1979

Clarke, R., *A Whisper of God*, Dublin: The Columba Press, 2006

Condren, M., *The Serpent and the Goddess*, San Francisco: Harper and Row, 1989

Congregation for Divine Worship, *Defending the Faith*, http://www.cfpeople.org/Books/GIRM/GIRMp11.htm

Cunneen, S., *In Search of Mary: The Woman and the Symbol*, New York: Ballantine Books, 1996

Cunningham, L., 'Born of a Woman (Gal 4:4): A Theological Meditation' in C. E. Braaten and R.W. Jenson (eds), *Mary Mother of God*, Cambridge: Eerdmans, 2004, pp 36-48

Daly, M., *Beyond God the Father*, Boston: Beacon Press, 1973

— *The Church and the Second Sex*, London: Geoffrey Chapman, 1968

Daly, C., 'Mary and the Church' in J. Hyland (ed), *Mary in the Church*, Dublin: Veritas, 1989, pp 131-141

De Beauvoir, S., *The Second Sex*, New York: Vintage Books, 1974

Donnelly, J. S., 'The Marian Shrine of Knock: The First Decade', *Éire-Ireland*, Vol XXVIII, No 2 (1993), pp 55-99

Drumm, M., and Gunning, T., A Sacramental People Vol 1, Dublin: The Columba Press, 1999

Elizondo, V., 'Our Lady of Guadalupe as a Cultural Symbol: The Power of the Powerless', *Concilium*, Vol 2, (1977), pp 25-33

Epiphanius, Panarion in Philip R. Amidon (ed), *The Panarion of St Epiphanius, Bishop of Salamis: Selected Passages 79.1., 79.9.3*, Oxford: OUP, 1990, pp 353-354

Farrell, M., 'The Assumption of Mary – Prophetic Symbol for a Pilgrim People', *The Australasian Catholic Record*, Vol LXIX, No 3 (1992), pp 320-331

Flanagan, D., 'The Veneration of Mary: A New Papal Document', *The Furrow*, Vol 25, No 5 (1974), pp 272-277

Graef, H., *Mary: A History of Doctrine and Devotion*, Vol 1, New York: Sheed and Ward, 1963

— *Mary: A History of Doctrine and Devotion*, Vol 2, New York: Sheed and Ward, 1965

Grassi, J., *Mary, Mother & Disciple*, Wilmington: Michael Glazier Inc, 1988

Hamington, M., *Hail Mary?* New York: Routledge, 1995

Hampson, D., *Theology and Feminism*, Massachusetts: Basil Blackwell, 1990

Harrington, W., *Mark*, Dublin: Veritas, 1979

Harris, R., *Lourdes: Body and the Spirit in the Secular Age*, London: Penguin, 1999

Heaney, S., *The Cure at Troy*, London: Faber and Faber, 1990

Hebblethwaite, P., 'The Mariology of Three Popes', *The Way*, Vol 51, (1984), pp 63-67

Hellwig, M., 'The Dogmatic Implications of the Birth of the Messiah', *Emmanuel*, Vol 84, (1978), pp.21-24

Hembrow Snyder, M., *The Christology of Rosemary Radford Ruether*, Mystic CT: Twenty Third Publications, 1988

Hogan, L., *From Women's Experience to Feminist Theology*, Sheffield: Sheffield Academic Press, 1995

Ishara, 'The Virgin Mary Isis of the Third Millennium'? [online] http://www.angelfire.com/realm2/amethystbt/MaryIsis.html

John XXIII, *Pacem in terris*, London: Catholic Truth Society, 1963

John Paul II, 'At the Root of the Eucharist is the Virginal and Maternal Life of Mary', *L'Osservatore Romano*, 24/788 (1983), pp 11-12

— 'Mary is the Greatest Success of the Paschal Mystery', *L'Osservatore Romano*, Vol 17, No 781 (1983), p 2

— *Mary Mother of the Redeemer*, Dublin: Veritas, 1987

— *Mulieris dignitatem*, London: Catholic Truth Society, 1988

— 'The Magnificat Answers Questions on Evangelizing', *L'Osservatore Romano*, Vol 9, No 950 (1979), p 3

— 'Uphold Dignity of Motherhood', *L'Osservatore Romano*, Vol 3, No 564 (1979), pp 1-9

Johnson, E., 'Mary and the Female Face of God', *Theological Studies*, Vol 50, (1989), pp 500-526

— *She Who Is: The Mystery of God in Feminist Theological Discourse*, New York: Crossroad, 1993

— *Friends of God and Prophets: A Feminist Theological Reading of the Communion of Saints*, New York: Continuum, 1998

— 'The Symbolic Character of Theological Statements about Mary', *Journal of Ecumenical Studies*, Vol 22, (1985), pp 312-336.
— *Truly Our Sister*, New York: Continuum, 2003
— 'Jesus the Wisdom of God: A Biblical Basis for Non-Androcentric Christology', *Ephemerides Thologicae Lovanienses*, Vol 61, No 4 (1985), pp 261-294

Kelly, B., 'Our Lady and Objective Redemption', *Irish Theological Quarterly*, Vol XXXIII, No 3 (1966), pp 242-353

Kelly, J. N. D., *Golden Mouth: The Story of John Chrysostom – Ascetic, Preacher, Bishop*, Ithaca: Cornell University Press, 1995

Kennedy, G. A., 'Good Friday Falls on Lady Day', *The Unutterable Beauty*, London: Hodder and Stoughton, 1947, p 98

Küng, H., *On Being a Christian*, London: Collins, 1974

Lane, D., *Christ at the Centre*, Dublin: Veritas, 1990
— *Foundations for a Social Theology*, Dublin: Gill and Macmillan, 1984
— *The Reality of Jesus*, Dublin: Veritas, 1975

Laurentin, R., and Lejeune, R., *Messages and Teachings of Mary at Medjugorje*, Ohio: Riehle Foundation, 1988

Laurentin, R., The *Apparitions of the Blessed Virgin Mary Today*, Dublin: Veritas, 1990

Leahy, B., *The Marian Profile*, London: New City, 2000

Loades, A., 'The Virgin Mary and the Feminist Quest' in J. Soskice (ed), *After Eve*, London: Collins, 1990, pp 156-178

Mackey, J., 'The use and abuse of Mary in Roman Catholicism' in Holloway (ed), *Who Needs Feminism?* London: SPCK, 1991, pp 99-116

Macquarrie, J., *Mary for all Christians*, London: Collins, 1991

Maeckelberghe, E., *Desperately Seeking Mary*, Kampen: Kok Pharos, 1991

Maher, M., 'A Break with Tradition: Ordaining Women Rabbis', *Irish Theological Quarterly*, Vol 72 (2007), pp 32-60

Malone, M. T., *Women and Christianity: The First Thousand Years, Vol 1*, Dublin: The Columba Press, 2000
— *Women and Christianity: The Medieval Period Vol 2, AD 1000-1500*, Dublin: The Columba Press, 2001
— *Women and Christianity: From the Reformation to the 21st Century Vol 3*, Dublin: The Columba Press, 2003

Maloney, C., *Mary*, Dublin: Gill and Son, 1936

Maunder, C., 'Apparitions of Mary' in S. Boss (ed), *Mary the Complete Resource*, New York: OUP, 2007, pp 424-457

Meier, J., *Matthew*, New Testament Message Vol 3, Dublin: Veritas, 1980

Miles, M., 'Roundtable Discussion Feminist Religious History', *Journal of Feminist Studies in Religion*, Vol 22, No 1 (2006), pp 45-74

Moltmann, J., 'Editorial: Can there be an ecumenical Mariology'? *Concilium*, Vol 168, (1983), pp XII-XV

Murphy, C., *Woman as Church*, Dublin: Gill and Macmillan, 1997

McBrien, R., *Catholicism*, San Francisco: Harper San Francisco, 1994

McCaslin, S., 'Mary Mother', *Journal of Feminist Studies in Religion*, Vol 23, No.1 (2007), pp 50-51

McEnroy, C., *Guests in Their Own House*, New York: Crossroad, 1996

McFague, S., *Models of God*, London: SCM Press, 1987.

McNamara, J. A. K., *Sisters in Arms*, Massachusetts: Harvard UP, 1992

McPhillips, K., 'Speaking Out: Gathering Women in the Postcolonial Pacific Region', *Journal of Feminist Studies in Religion*, Vol 23, No.1 (2007), pp 117-120

Novak, M., *The Open Church*, London: DLT, 1964

Osiek, C., *Beyond Anger*, Dublin: Gill and Macmillan, 1986

O'Carroll, M., 'Mary Mother of God' in J. Komonchak, M. Collins, D. Lane (eds), *The New Dictionary of Theology*, Dublin: Gill and Macmillan, 1987, pp 637-643

— *Mediatress of all Graces*, Dublin: Golden Eagle Books, 1959

— O'Carroll, M., *Theotokos*, Wilmington: Glazier, 1982

O'Donnell, C., *At Worship With Mary*, Delaware: Michael Glazier, 1988

O'Grady, M., 'Mary's Role in Redemption' in K. McNamara (ed), *Mother of the Redeemer*, Dublin: Gill and Son, 1959, pp 135-158

O'Loughlin, T., *Marian Encyclical*, Dublin: Veritas, 1987

Pannenberg, W., 'Mary, Redemption, and Unity', *Una Sancta*, Vol 24, No 1 (1967), pp 62-68

Paredes, J., *Mary and the Kingdom of God*, Middlegreen: St Paul Publications, 1990

Parker, M., *Seamus Heaney: The Making of the Poet*, Basingstoke: University of Iowa Press, 1993

Patrick, A., 'Toward Renewing the Life and Culture of Fallen Man: *Gaudium et spes* as Catalyst for Catholic Feminist Theology' in J. Dwyer (ed), *Questions of Special Urgency*, Washington DC: Georgetown University Press, 1986, pp 55-78

Paul VI, *Marialis cultus*, Vatican City: Vatican Polyglot Press, 1974

— 'Declaration on the Question of Admission of Women to the Ministerial Priesthood' http://www.papalencyclicals.net/ Paul06/ index.htm

— *Octogesima adveniens* in M. Walsh and B. Davies (eds), *Proclaiming Justice and Peace*, London: Collins Liturgical Publications, 1984

Pelikan, J., *Mary Through the Centuries*, New Haven: Yale UP, 1996

Pius IX., 'Apostolic Constitution of Pope Pius IX on the Immaculate Conception (December 8, 1854)' http://www.newadvent.org/ library/docs_pi09id.htm

Pius XII, *Munificentissimus Deus*, Dublin: Irish Messenger Office, 1950

— *Mystici Corporis*, New York: The America Press, 1943

— 'Mediator Dei: Encyclical of Pope Pius XII on the Sacred Liturgy to the Venerable Brethren, the Patriarchs, Primates, Archbishops, Bishops [sic] and Other Ordinaries in Peace and Communion with the Apostolic See' http://www.vatican.va/holy_father/ pius_xii/ encyclicals/ documents/hf_p-xii_enc_ 20111947_ mediator-dei_en. html

Porter, F., *It Will Not Be Taken Away From Her*, London: DLT, 2004

Quasten, J., *Patrology*, Utrecht: Spectrum Publishers, 1966

Rahner, K., 'Christology Today', *Theological Investigations* Vol 21, London: DLT, 1988, pp 220-227

— 'The Immaculate Conception', *Theological Investigations* Vol 1, London: DLT,, 1965, pp 201-203

— 'The Interpretation of the Dogma of the Assumption', *Theological Investigations* Vol 1, London: DLT, 1965, pp 215-227

— *Visions and Prophecies*, London: Burns and Oates, 1963

Ross, S. A., 'Church and sacrament – community and worship' in S. F. Parsons (ed), *The Cambridge Companion to Feminist Theology*, Cambridge: CUP, 2002, pp 224-242

Rubin, M., *Mother of God: A History of the Virgin Mary*, London: Allen Lane, 2009

Ruether, R., 'Can Christology be Liberated from Patriarchy?' in M. Stevens (ed), *Reconstructing the Christ Symbol: Essays in Feminist Christology*, New York: Paulist Press, 1993, pp 7-29

— 'Consciousness Raising at Puebla', *Christianity and Crisis*, Vol 39, (1979), pp 77-79

— 'Male Clericalism and the Dread of Women' *Ecumenist*, Vol 11, (1973), pp 65-69

— *Mary – The Feminine Face of the Church*, London: Westminster Press, 1977

— *Sexism and God-Talk*, London: SCM Press, 1983

— 'The Interrelatedness of Oppression and Efforts for Liberation: A Feminist Perspective' in V. Fabella and S. Torres (eds), *Doing Theology in a Divided World*, New York: Orbis Books, 1985, pp 65-71

— *To Change the World*, London: SCM, 1981

Russell, L., *Church in the Round*, Louisville: Westminster/John Knox Press, 1993

Rutt, R., 'Why should he send his Mother? Some theological reflections on Marian apparitions' in W. McLoughlin and J. Pennock (eds), *Mary is for Everyone*, Herefordshire: Gracewing, 1997, pp 274-284

Sacred Congregation for Divine Worship, *General Norms for the Liturgical Year and Calendar*, M. A. Simcoe (ed), Chicago: Liturgy Training Publications, 1985, pp 179-195

Schaberg, J., *The Illegitimacy of Jesus: A Feminist Theological Interpretation of the Infancy Narratives*, San Francisco: Harper and Row, 1987

Schneiders, S., *Beyond Patching*, New York: Paulist Press, 1991

Schüssler Fiorenza, E., 'Feminist studies in religion and a radical democratic ethos' http://www.unisa.ac.za/default.asp? Cmd=ViewContent&ContentID=7347

Semmelroth, O., *Mary the Archetype of the Church*, Dublin: Gill & Son, 1964

Spretnak, C., *Missing Mary*, New York: Palgrave Macmillan, 2004

Stacpoole, A., 'Mary in Ecumenical Dialogue' in J. Hyland (ed), *Mary in the Church*, Dublin: Veritas, 1989, pp 57-78

Synod of Bishops, *Theology of Justice in the World 3*, Vatican City: Pontifical Biblical Commission for Justice and Peace, 1971

Tambasco, A., *What are they saying about Mary?* New York: Paulist Press, 1984

Tavard, G., *The Thousand Faces of the Virgin Mary*, Collegeville MN: The Liturgical Press, 1996

Treanor, O., *Mary Mother of the Redeemer Mother of the Redeemed*, Guernsey: Guernsey Press Co Ltd, 1988

Untener, K., 'Forum: The Ordination of Women. Can Horizons Widen'? *Worship*, Vol 65, No 1 (1991), pp 50-59

Vatican Council II, *Gaudium et spes* in *The Counciliar and Post Counciliar Documents*, A. Flannery (ed), Dublin: Dominican Publications, 1975

— *Lumen gentium* in *The Counciliar and Post Counciliar Documents*, A. Flannery (ed), Dublin: Dominican Publications, 1975

— *Sacrosanctum concilium* in *The Counciliar and Post Counciliar Documents*, A. Flannery (ed), Dublin: Dominican Publications, 1975

— *Unitatis redintegratio* in *The Counciliar and Post Counciliar Documents*, A. Flannery (ed), Dublin: Dominican Publications, 1975

Vawter, B., 'The Gospel According to John' in R. Brown, J. Fitzmyer and R. Murphy (eds), *The Jerome Biblical Commentary*, London: Geoffrey Chapman, 1981, pp 414-466

Vollert, C., *A Theology of Mary*, Herder and Herder: New York, 1965

Von Balthasar, H., *The Office of Peter and the Structure of the Church*, San Francisco: Ignatius Press, 1986

Warner, M., *Alone of All Her Sex*, London: Pan Books, 1976

Wicks, J., 'A Commentary on Mary: Grace and Hope in Christ of the Anglican-Roman Catholic International Commission – 2005' http://www.vatican.va/roman_curia/pontifical_councils/?chrstu ni/angl-comm-docs/rc_